For my dear lo⟨⟩ W9-AEA-307
    who has the biggest and
the best heart —

        Love from Phyllis
            Christmas 1984

FOLK HEARTS

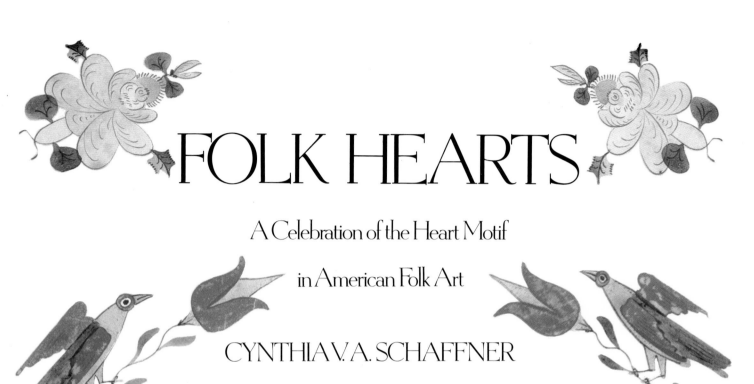

FOLK HEARTS

A Celebration of the Heart Motif

in American Folk Art

CYNTHIA V. A. SCHAFFNER

and SUSAN KLEIN

Alfred A. Knopf

New York 1984

THIS IS A BORZOI BOOK
PUBLISHED BY ALFRED A. KNOPF, INC.

The following photographs were taken by Schecter Lee: Figures 2, 3, 5, 6, 9, 10, 22, 23, 28, 29, 30, 31, 34, 35, 36, 38, 48, 49, 51, 52, 53, 54, 55, 57, 63, 64, 65, 67, 73, 74, 76, 77, 78, 79, 80, 81, 82, 83, 84, 85, 88, 90, 91, 92, 93, 94, 95, 96, 97, 102, 103, 104, 105A&B, 111, 112, 113, 114, 115, 116, 117, 124, 125, 126, 127, 128, 129, 130, 132, 133, 134, 135, 138, 141, 144, 147, 148A&B, and the photograph on page viii. © by Schecter Lee.

The following photographs were taken by Bill Holland: Figures 12, 13, 14, 15, 16, 18, 19, 20, 21, 24, 25, 27, 32, 39, 43, 56, 59, 66, 89, 107, 108, 109, 122, 125, 140, 150. © by Bill Holland.

The following photographs are reproduced by courtesy of E. P. Dutton: Figures 33, 58, 60, 87, 131.

Library of Congress Cataloging in Publication Data
Main entry under title: Folk hearts.
1. Folk art—United States—Themes, motives. 2. Heart in art. I. Schaffner, Cynthia V. A. II. Klein, Susan,
NK806.F64   1984   745′0973   84-47783
ISBN 0-394-53496-4

Manufactured in Japan

First Edition

To Bob and Hilary
and
To Robert, Andy, and Jeffrey

Contents

"Heart and crown" armchair. The initials "A.G." are carved in the back of the center heart. Framington-Avon, Simsbury area, Connecticut. (*Lillian Blankley Cogan Collection*)

Acknowledgments

SEARCHING for folk hearts, researching their origins, and discovering the spirit of their creation has involved many people we would like to acknowledge.

We extend a special thanks to Gerard C. Wertkin, who offered us invaluable advice throughout the research and writing of the book, and read and critiqued our text. To Frederick S. Weiser our appreciation for guiding our understanding of Pennsylvania German Fraktur. To Betsy Garrett our warmest thanks for continually pointing us in new directions. And to Marie DiManno our gratitude for her enthusiasm and for getting us started.

Our heartfelt thanks also go to the many friends, collectors, dealers, and scholars who shared with us their expertise, enthusiasm, hospitality and collections: Linda and Irwin Berman; Bill Bernard; Dr. Robert Bishop; Joyce Black; Catherine G. Cahill; Cathie Calvert; Trudy Champe; Patricia Coblentz; Barry Cohen; Lillian Blankley Cogan; Father Walter L. Creahen; Ellisa Cullman; David P. and Susan M. Cunningham; Phillip Curtis; Alan L. Daniel; Christina Davis; Lucy Danziger; Davida Deutsch; Nancy Druckman; Adele Earnst; Mary Jaene Edmonds; Elaine Eff; Ralph Esmerian; Daniel and Jessie Lie Farber; Howard and Catherine Feldman; Helaine and Burton Fendelman; Susan Flamm; Leslie Gaines; Wendell Garrett; Dona Guimarães; Jay Gaynor; Harriet Griffin; Blanche Greenstein; Lillian and Jerry Grossman; Helen Haroutunian; Herbert W. Hemphill, Jr.; Jonathan Holstein; Joan and Victor Johnson; Dorothy Kaufman; Joel and Kate Kopp: America Hurrah Antiques, New York City; Libby Kramer; Prof. John K. Lattimer; Jo Carole and Ronald Lauder; Wendy Lavitt; Jean Lipman; Sara Lindberg; Richard S. and Rosemarie B. Machmer; Gayle Malles; Mr. and Mrs. Foster McCarl, Jr.; Mr. and Mrs. William Moore; Charles Muller; Cyril I. Nelson; Doreen Paloucci; Sheila and Edwin Rideout; Betty Ring; Joanna S. Rose; George E. Schoelkopf; Karen Schuster; Sanford and Patricia Smith; Nancy and Gary Stass; Betty Sterling; Scott Swank; Doris and Stanley Tananbaum; Gail van der Hoof; Judith R. Weissman;

Tom Woodard; Thos. K. Woodard: American Antiques and Quilts, New York City; Donald Walters; Susan Waterfall; and Riki and Gene Zuriff.

Many institutions were involved in our search. The Abby Aldrich Rockefeller Folk Art Center, Williamsburg, Virginia: Barbara Luck; Cooper-Hewitt Museum, The Smithsonian Institution's National Museum of Design, New York: Gillian Moss, Cordelia Rose and Carmel Wilson; Franklin and Marshall College Collections, Lancaster, Pennsylvania: Carol Faill; Hallmark Historical Collection, Hallmark Card, Inc., Sally A. Hopkins; Hancock Shaker Village, Pittsfield, Massachusetts: Tom Harrington; Heritage Center of Lancaster, Lancaster, Pennsylvania: Bruce Shoemaker and Cynthia Wiley; The Metropolitan Museum of Art, New York; The Museum of the City of New York, New York: Jennifer Bright; The National Museum of American History, Smithsonian Institution, Washington, D.C.: Anne Serio; New York State Historical Association, Cooperstown, New York: Kathy Stocking; Old Sturbridge Village, Sturbridge, Massachusetts; Philadelphia Museum of Art, Philadelphia, Pennsylvania: Ann Bixler and Gail Tomlinson; Rockford-Kauffman Museum: Ann Taylor. And we extend a special thanks to the trustees, staff, docents, and Friends of the Museum of American Folk Art—our "home away from home."

To our editor, Alice Quinn, our deepest thanks for her patience, advice, and for her special affinity for the spirit of *Folk Hearts.* Our admiration and joy to Schecter Lee, whose magnificent photographs bring a new vision to the heart motif. Our thanks, too, to Bill Holland for his photographs from Pennsylvania collections. And to Michelle Marino who typed the manuscript.

A special thanks to Margaret Wagner for her wonderful design, and to Peggy Rauch and Ellen McNeilly for their prodigious efforts in overseeing the production of the book.

And to our families....From Cynthia: My deepest affection to my husband Bob and my daughter, Hilary, for their unfailing support and encouragement; and to my parents, Abigail H. and James A. Van Allen, for their example and for always being there. From Susan: A few people played a special role in the evolution of this project. My special love and thanks to my husband, Robert, and my sons, Andy and Jeffrey. My deepest gratitude to my friend Mimi Barton, for her guidance, and to my parents, Rhoda and Alfred Tananbaum, who have enriched my life and to whom I owe so much.

FOLK HEARTS

1. A majestic cut-work valentine, c. 1790. Note how the wings of the doves frame the corner hearts. Possibly New York. 11¾″ l. x 11½″ w. (*Courtesy of the Museum of the City of New York*)

I
INTRODUCTION

THE folk art of America from the seventeenth to the late nineteenth century depicts a variety of traditional motifs. The heart—a universal symbol of secular and religious love, courage, and friendship, hospitality, loyalty, and fidelity—is one of the most enchanting.

Itinerant artists painted hearts on dower chests and birth and baptismal certificates. Young girls stitched and embroidered hearts on samplers and quilts; tinsmiths pierced hearts in foot warmers; potters etched them on presentation plates. Puritan stonecutters carved hearts on gravestones, and carpenters and craftsmen carved out and drew hearts on furniture, including chests and chairs. The heart shape was painted on paper by traveling artists, schoolmasters, and ministers; ironmongers wrought heart shapes on kitchen utensils, and sailors incised hearts on whale's teeth during their long voyages in search of the great sperm whales.

Hearts were glazed onto stoneware, woven into coverlets and cut out from paper. All these products of brush, kiln, loom, needle, and scissors were born out of need, but they were embellished to please the eye of the maker and to kindle feelings in the beholder. They were the personal expression of both men and women—folk artists who were by nature, rather than by training, masters of their craft.

Often things adorned with a heart were given as tokens of friendship and affection. They combine an intimacy that is compelling, a self-consciousness that is appealing, and an individuality that imparts a treasured quality to each item.

Hearts were a traditional symbolic motif often associated with the folk art surrounding the major events of life: birth, marriage, and death. It is in the home that most of these objects were found. Many were used for "best" or for "company"; they became family heirlooms, carefully saved generation after generation. Love letters were tucked away, but wedding gifts were often displayed prominently, and rarely thrown away or left behind. All of these now provide us with a body of splendid work to draw upon—the record of a design form and of an entire way of life.

It is generally thought that America's folk art flowered after the Revolutionary War, when colonists were freed from the taxing labors of bare survival and experienced a new level of prosperity and confidence. This is also true of the heart motif, but to ignore the period before the war would be to delete an important chapter in its development. The heart was a borrowed motif—English and other European settlers were largely responsible for bringing it to American folk art. Though scarce, the early objects document this transference. As early as 1674, a gravestone cutter carved a heart on a tombstone in Charlestown, Massachusetts. A blacksmith cut out a heart, a clover leaf, and the date 1682 on a banner weather vane that stood on the roof of the second meetinghouse in Lynn, Massachusetts. The first American sampler is attributed to Lora Standish, daughter of Miles Standish, dating from the 1640s. Although Lora's sampler does not have a graphic depiction of a heart, the following verse is stitched:

2. The clenched fist atop a crown of four hearts made a comfortable grip for this scrimshaw bodkin. c. 1850. 3¼″ h. (*Collection of Barbara Johnson*)

Laora [*sic*] Standish is my name
Lorde Guide My Hart That
I May Doe they Will also Fill
My Hands With Such con-
Venient Skil as May
Conduce to Vertue Void of
Shame and I Will Give
Glory to they name[1]

During the last quarter of the seventeenth century, elegant hearts adorned Hadley-type chests in western Massachusetts, and "heart and crown" chairs in coastal Connecticut.

The period after the death of George Washington in 1799 was one of great sentimentality in America, and this was reflected in the folk arts. Particularly after 1820, the heart became an increasingly sentimental motif, associated primarily with romance and friendship, and moving away from the transplanted religious, allegorical, and traditional meaning brought by the Europeans. By the last quarter of the nineteenth century industrialization had reached all but the most remote areas of the country, changing the original spirit in which folk art was created. While the folk arts in America continued to flourish, the 1880s provide a natural stopping point for this study of the celebration of the heart motif in American folk art.

3. The Harman Fonda–
Rachel Lansing family
record. Watercolor and
ink by William Murray,
Mohawk Valley, New
York. Dated 31 August,
1819. 16″ h. x 12″ w.
(Private Collection. Pho-
tograph courtesy of Amer-
ica Hurrah Antiques,
New York City)

4. Religious text attributed to the Mennonite schoolmaster Martin Gottshall, 1835–45. The heart-shaped angels, the peacocks, and the staunch ladies guarding the central heart below make this one of the most graphically beautiful of Frakturs. Ink and watercolor on paper. Montgomery County, Pennsylvania. 12″ h. x 7¾″ w. *(Private Collection)*

II
HEART HISTORY

THE bold form and appealing grace of the simple heart design echo an ancient motif, with hazy origins and a fascinating history. The design has roots reaching back twenty thousand years. A great heart was found on a painting of a mammoth in the caves of Cro-Magnon man.[1] Almost every ancient religion and culture throughout the world has attributed to the heart important symbolic significance. The Chinese, Hindu, Judaic, Christian, and Islamic religions all viewed the heart as the center of life, the soul or spirit of man. Thus the heart, with interesting variations, became an object related to the veneration of God.

The organ constantly beating and located in the center of the body was easily exalted as a symbol of life itself. The earliest medical discussions of the heart are found in the Old Egyptian *Ebers* papyrus of 1500 B.C., which describes how the blood vessels lead from the heart throughout the body. The Egyptians thought that the heart sent messages along the blood-stream, directing all bodily actions. Thus they concluded that the heart was the organ of thought and the seat of intelligence.[2] Greek philosophers and physicians agreed. Aristotle believed the heart to be the source of man's thought and emotions and the controlling agent of the rest of the body. Plato located the soul of man in his heart and made it the ruler of both intelligence and emotions.

The Old Testament associates fainting, death, and longevity with the heart, and regards it metaphorically as the source of man's intellectual activities and the controller of thought, will, feeling, and consciousness. The New Testament is replete with references to the heart; it is to be the dwelling place of Christ, in which resides the peace of God.

In many cultures the heart was given special attention at death. The ancient Egyptians removed the organ for mummification, placing it in a scarab that often contained the in-scription: "On my heart confess not against me as a witness."[3] The Egyptian Book of the Dead depicts the heart, symbol of will, at the judgment scene—balanced on a scale with a feather, symbol of law. The text beside it reads:

5. Pewter chatelaine, c. 1800–20. Worn at the waist and used to carry sewing implements or trinkets. Possibly Pennsylvania. 2″ l. (*Collection of Nancy and Gary Stass*)

"Heart mine of my mother! Heart mine of my existence (upon earth)! Let there be no estoppel [*sic*] against me through adverse evidence. Let there be no hindrance to me through the Divine Powers. Let not there be a fall of the scale against me in presence of him who presides at the Balance."[4]

In this depiction, the heart is oval. In others it appears in the shape of a keystone or inside of an urn.

The Aztecs in Mexico removed hearts from sacrificial victims, ritualistically offering them to the gods and then burning and burying them. In some American Indian cultures the heart of a brave man or a ferocious animal was eaten in the belief that courage and bravery could be acquired thereby. Greek mythology contains various versions of the death of Dionysius, who was eaten by the Titans, but whose heart was rescued and brought to Zeus; thus making possible his rebirth. In medieval Europe, separate heart burial was common practice. And many poems, ballads, legends, and myths throughout history are filled with tales of hearts magically exchanged or tragically lost.

The heart shape as we know it today can be found in Egyptian art dating from the fourteenth century B.C.; it was part of the distinctive decoration painted on Egyptian coffins. Later, hearts appear on Coptic embroidery—possibly as religious symbols. It is the Egyptians who have been credited with bringing the heart form to Europe in the sixth century A.D.[5]

In European Christian art, the heart more closely resembled the anatomical organ, with a rounded bottom and a cusp at the top. Often it appeared in association with other symbols—as a flaming heart, or one pierced by arrows, or on a cross surrounded by a crown of thorns. These symbols were also commonly used as attributes of various saints. Religious hearts were red, signifying divine love. Red was also associated with Donar, the god of marriage and the home in Germanic mythology. During the fifteenth century, Leonardo da Vinci carefully studied and sketched the heart and described the circulation of the blood, but his efforts as a medical scientist went largely unnoticed.

The Middle Ages, from the sixth century to the middle of the fifteenth, witnessed a dramatic evolution of culture, art, and language throughout Europe. From this period there are scattered clues as to the directions that the heart design would take in the flowering of folk art in the seventeenth and eighteenth centuries. Medieval iconography drew heavily from the scriptures for inspiration. The heart representing the love of God was used in the ornamentation and architecture of cathedrals and in association with other symbols and specific saints in paintings and sculpture.

When Parisian cardmakers at the end of the fourteenth century introduced the first set of playing cards using the now familiar suits—hearts, diamonds, spades, and clubs—each suit was thought to represent one of the four classes of French medieval society at the time.[6] Hearts were then associated with the ecclesiastical hierarchy. The English adopted all four suits, but the Germans and other northern Europeans chose only the heart, preferring bells, leaves, and acorns for the remaining suits.[7] Their selection reflected a different source of tradition, drawing from symbols associated with growth, fertility, regeneration. The heart, the source from which all things grow, becomes in folk art of the eighteenth century a symbol of Mother Earth. Flowers growing from a heart were a common motif in northern European textiles, particularly in the seventeenth and eighteenth centuries.[8]

The romantic medieval tradition of courtly and chivalric love had begun using the heart as a symbol of secular love by the twelfth century. The celebration of the spring festival of St. Valentine derives from the Roman mating festivals of Lupercalia. Church fathers gave these popular festivals the name of a Christian saint in an effort to eliminate all pagan Roman traditions. In the twelfth and thirteenth centuries the heart was associated with romantic love in French ballads which told of troubadours offering their hearts to fair maidens.[9] In the fifteenth-century illuminated manuscript *Book of Love* (*Le Cueur d'amours éspris*), written by Duc René of Anjou, the red heart appears as a valentine shape—its two lobes rounded at the top, and pointed at the bottom.[10] The heart was also found on woven carpets, on carvings in ivory, and on jewelry boxes of this period.[11]

The Medieval Collection at the Metropolitan Museum of Art in New York City displays a fourteenth-century coffret or covered box with painted and gilded scenes of love and courtship. One side of the box includes a seated male figure presenting a red, valentine-shaped heart to his lady.[12]

This collection also includes a French boxwood comb from the fifteenth century with a carved valentine-shaped heart pierced by one arrow. Red hearts and cut-out hearts embellished the shields, lances, facepieces, and halberds of sixteenth- and seventeenth-century court armor and regalia. In tournaments and festive processions, they symbolized a lover's chivalry.[13]

By the time of the Renaissance, parts of Europe had changed from an agricultural, feudal society to the beginnings of an industrial, modern one. Art, literature, and learning, particularly in the sixteenth century, altered forever man's concept of himself and the pivotal importance of God's relationship to man. Philosophers and scientists transformed the concept of the heart as the center of both intelligence and emotion, focusing on the brain as the center of

6. Wrought-iron trivet. Probably Pennsylvania. c. 1775–1800. 10″ l. x 5″ w. (*Collection of Nancy and Gary Stass*)

thinking and reasoning, and the heart as the center of the emotions. Martin Luther in Germany and John Calvin in Switzerland brought about the Reformation, which challenged the doctrines and authority of the Catholic Church and established Protestantism. Both men adopted the heart in their seals.

In Middle English, the written language in Britain during the twelfth to fifteenth centuries, "heort," "herte," and "hart" were three common forms of spelling as the meanings greatly expanded. The printing press in the fifteenth century gave enormous impetus to the codification of the English language, and in 1775 Samuel Johnson's *Dictionary of the English Language* listed the word with twenty-one definitions, opening with the following:

> Heart. 1. The muscle which by its contraction and dilation propels the blood through the course of circulation, and is therefore considered as the source of vital motion. 2. It is supposed in popular language to be the seat sometimes of courage, sometimes of affection, sometimes of honesty, or baseness. 3. The chief part; the vital part; the vigorous or officacious part. 4. The inner part of any thing. 5. Person; character; used with respect to courage or kindness. 6. Courage; Spirit. 7. Seat of love. 8. Affection; inclination.[14]

Folk art flourished in the eighteenth century. Craftsmen had gained a new degree of independence and affluence, allowing for the richer embellishment of their homes and objects of daily use. And they adopted familiar and traditional motifs, perhaps copying without an understanding of its meaning the religious iconography of the past. Thus the heart became as much associated with man's love as with God's love, finding expression in painted furniture, textiles, embroidery, and objects of daily use. Throughout the British Isles, France, Germany, Switzerland, Austria, Hungary, Holland, and Scandinavia, the heart became associated with the traditions and customs surrounding courtship and marriage.

7. Walnut child's chair. Lancaster, Pennsylvania. c. 1750. 34″ h. (Photo courtesy of The Magazine *Antiques*)

Hearts adorned love tokens and the gifts of courtship—mangle boards, clothes beaters, weaver's reeds, bedsticks, clock cases, rolling pins, and boxes. Blacksmiths punched hearts in lanterns, kettles, tools, and foot warmers. Shepherds whittled hearts on walking sticks during idle hours. Hearts were used on the furniture of the bride's dowry—dower chests, marriage boxes, spoon shelves, and wooden chairs. The heart was used on cut-paper designs in Switzerland, Austria, and Alsace, and on illuminated manuscripts in Germany. In America early settlers carried on the traditional use of this motif, which flourished in the folk art of the seventeenth, eighteenth, and nineteenth centuries.

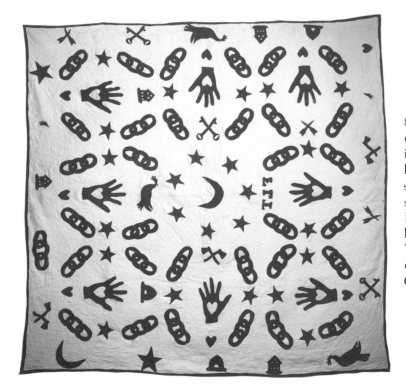

8. Odd Fellows or Masons quilt, chock-full of symbolic imagery: crossed hatchets, keys, arrows, linked chains, sliver moons, five-pointed stars, and hearts-in-hand. For good measure: a hen, a house, and a beehive. Vermont. 19th century. 69″ square. (*Joanna S. Rose Collection*)

9. Foot warmer with twenty hearts, made of pierced tin and wood and filled with hot coals. Mainly used for outings—in the sleigh, in church, or in a meeting house. A popular wedding gift. Pennsylvania. 9″ l. x 7½″ d. x 6″ h. (*Collection of Mr. and Mrs. Eugene Zuriff*)

10. Salt-glazed stoneware flask, inscribed with the name of the recipient. Cornwall, New York, dated September 1860. 7¾″ h. *(Barry Cohen Collection)*

are lyes

11. Slate tombstone of Peter Ripley, dated 1742. Hingham, Massachusetts. 27″ h. *(Photograph courtesy of Daniel and Jessie Lie Farber)*

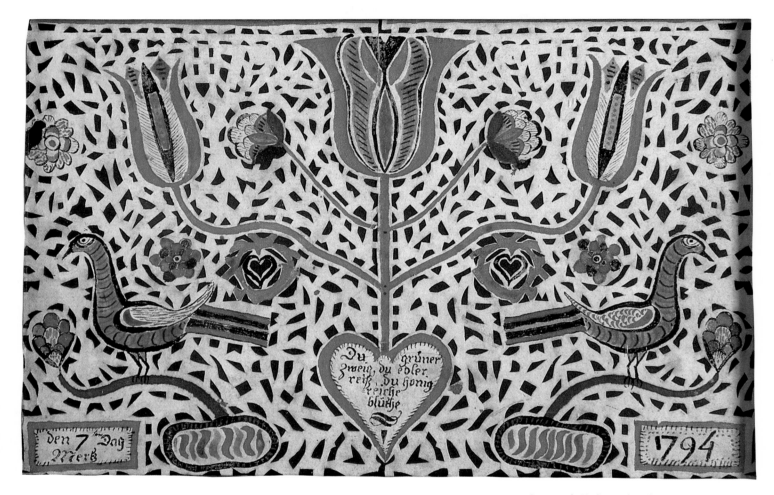

13. Watercolor and ink calling card by the "Heart and Hand" artist. New Hampshire. c. 1800–25. 4⅝″ h. x 4¼″ w. (*Howard and Catherine Feldman Collection*)

12. Cut-work Fraktur, dated 7 March 1794. Watercolor on paper. Artist unknown. Pennsylvania. 4½″ h. x 7⅛″ w. (*Howard and Catherine Feldman Collection*)

14. Birth and baptismal certificate for Wilhelm Portzline (born 7 October 1812), made by his father. Francis Portzline was the first Fraktur artist to be identified, and birds with heart-shaped wings are a hallmark of his style. Note the checkerboard feathers on the two middle birds—a mischievous improvement on nature! Pennsylvania. 1800–50. 12⅜″ h. x 15⅜″ w. (*Howard and Catherine Feldman Collection*)

III
HEARTS ON FRAKTUR

IN the Pennsylvania German culture of the eighteenth and nineteenth centuries, the arrival of a baby was recorded artistically on birth and baptismal certificates. Nowhere but in Pennsylvania do we find·such a large, homogeneous body of personal documents that glorify a child's entry into this world. These documents were part of the Fraktur tradition, which, as defined today, consists of a variety of illuminated texts written in pen, ink, and watercolor with Gothic lettering and ornamental designs. The most common type of Fraktur was the birth and baptismal certificate (Gerburts and Taufschein), but other examples include rewards of merit, house blessings (Haus-Segen), bookplates, writing samples (Vorschrift), religious broadsides, book illuminations, and valentines.

Immigrants from Switzerland, Alsace, and southwest Germany settled in southeastern Pennsylvania from 1683. They were Protestants from the Lutheran and Reformed churches, and they brought with them the tradition of birth and baptismal certificates. These documents listed the name of the new arrival, the name of his or her parents (including the mother's maiden name), the date and place of birth, often the hour of birth, and the zodiacal sign; then came the date of baptism, the baptizing pastor, the confession, and the sponsors. Accompanying this information were verses from hymns and whimsical designs.[1] The Pennsylvania German heart was a rounded, billowy, symmetrical form, executed either freehand or with a compass. Decoratively speaking, the heart became an expressive image of love with faint overtones of religious iconography. "Unless a religious character is asserted for these designs in their every manifestation," Pastor Frederick S. Weiser has written, "the simpler explanation is that they were employed for their inherent beauty and popular appeal."[2]

The heart was often drawn on the borders of certificates, and used as a central motif containing vital statistics or surrounding a religious text. A rare birth, baptismal, and confirmation record thoroughly emphasizing the heart motif was made for Abraham Kramer and

dated 1793 (fig. 22). The heart on a baptismal certificate might represent the source of love and faithfulness to God, thus encouraging piety. A certificate for Sara Seifer contains a common verse seen on tombstones and other Frakturs, stating that if the heart is pure it can belong to Jesus, secure from sin and temptation (fig. 27). The flat whimsical angels at the top are present as a warning of the announcement of the Last Judgment.[3] Many of the unknown artists, such as the one who executed this piece, were rural Lutheran and Reformed schoolmasters who taught hymn singing and religious classes.[4]

But there were also important Fraktur artists, known for their distinctive handling of the heart motif. Francis Portzline of Dauphin County, Pennsylvania (fig. 14), intertwined two hearts at the bottom of the central heart, and incorporated heart shapes in the wings of the two birds in the documents he decorated. And the man now known as the "Cumberland Valley Artist" created a motif of nine hearts (see fig. 15).

The birth and baptismal certificate for Rebecca Lindemuth (fig. 17) was executed by the "Stony Creek Artist" from Shenandoah Valley, Virginia. His design of a "heavenly curtain" further emphasizes the importance of the heart and the information it encloses. Several Frakturs made by this artist for members of the Lutheran and Reformed Zion congregations at Stony Creek have been found.

Additional examples of Fraktur such as house blessings, bookplates, religious broadsides, drawings, and writing samples were executed by the local schoolmaster, minister—whoever, proficient in penmanship, worked as a Fraktur artist. These pieces employed similar decorative motifs—flowers, birds, geometric patterns, and hearts. The bookplate in fig. 18 is colorfully decorated with the familiar tulip growing from the heart. Originally this was a graphic representation of the Protestant precept: From a pure heart good works develop. Here, however, the religious meaning is absent, and the tulip and heart are purely decorative. The bookplates were probably presented by schoolmasters to children as rewards for merit.

In fig. 20, the strong colors and stylized figures combined with bold heart are similar to the work in fig. 23. The religious text is attributed to Martin Gottshall, a member of a Mennonite religious sect in Montgomery County, Pennsylvania, that developed its own school of Fraktur. Martin and Samuel Gottshall and their father, Reverend Jacob Godshall, are all known for their illustrated drawings. The vision and skill of the Gottshalls and other inspired Fraktur makers elevate these personal documents to the realm of art.

15. Birth and baptismal certificate by Joseph Lochbaum, known as the "Nine Heart Artist" because every Fraktur by his hand contained nine hearts. Watercolor and ink on paper. Maryland or Pennsylvania. 1804. 13″ h. x 15½″ w. *(Private Collection)*

16. Pinprick and watercolor Fraktur, dated 1794. The fan-shaped flowers above the heart are made of hearts. Pennsylvania. 13¼″ h. x 16″ w. *(Howard and Catherine Feldman Collection)*

17. Birth and baptismal certificate, hand-drawn, -lettered, and -colored on laid paper by the man known as the "Stony Creek Artist" of Shenandoah County, Virginia. c. 1820. 9¾″ h. x 8¼″ w. (*Collection of the Rare Book Department, Free Library of Philadelphia. Photo courtesy of Arthur Soll*)

18. A Schwenkfelder or Mennonite book-plate from the Bally region of Pennysl-vania. The heart is inscribed in German: "This new spiritual songbook belongs to me Maria Larschar, 6th day of February, the year of our Lord 1786." 7½" h. x 4½" w. (*Private Collection*) ·

19. Birth and baptismal certificate for Daniel Braueflaeber of Lancaster County, Pennsylvania. Watercolor and ink on paper by Henry Young, known as "Reverend Young" perhaps because he was a church organist and a parochial schoolteacher. Dated 1827. 11¼″ h. 8¼″ w. *(Howard and Catherine Feldman Collection)*

20. Bookplate attributed to Samuel or Martin Gottshall, Montgomery County, Pennsylvania. In Protestant symbology, the heart becomes pure through faith, and from a pure heart arise good works. 1800–25. 6⅝″ h. x 4″ w. (*Howard and Catherine Feldman Collection*)

21. Bookplate for Barbara Grokin, dated 29 January 1812. The sculptural quality of the design is evocative of tombstone carvings. The wings open out as if they were tiers (or the ceiling) of a concert hall. Pennsylvania. 3⅝″ h. x 6⅜″ w. (*Howard and Catherine Feldman Collection*)

Diesen beyden Ehegatten, als Mstr. Lorenz Krämer und seiner ehelichen Haus-Frau Sophia Catharina eine gebohrne Jostin ist ein Sohn zur Welt gebohren, als Abraham Krämer ist zur Welt gebohren im Jahr unsers HErrn JEsu 1776. den 12. Tag Januari um Uhr im Zeichen de

GOTT gebe Gnad, Kraft und Stärke, daß dieser Abraham in der Furcht zum Lob und Preiß des HERRN möge aufwachsen und zunehmen in groser Begierde der vernünftigen lautern Milch, das ursprüngliche Heil der Seelen zu suchen, nach abgelegtem Glaubens-Bekänntniß und Erkäntniß der Sünde durch wahre Reu und Buße, vor der Christlichen Gemeinde, zur geistlichen Wiedergeburt der Heiligen Taufe befördert, und von Hrn: Conrad Röller Prediger und Diener des Worts, nach Christi Befehl, Mathäi 28, v. 19. getauft und in den Gnaden-Bund Gottes einverleibet worden. Dieser Abraham ist, als ein Glied in die Gemeinschaft der Heiligen, durch das Bad der Wiedergeburt und Erneuerung des Heiligen Geistes, wie St. Paulus lehret, Titum 3, v. 5. 6. 7. zu der lutger: Relig. ist auf- und angenommen worden, den 31-ten Tag Merz 1776. und durch den wahren Glauben an unsern Erlöser JEsu Christo, des so theuer erworbenen Verdienstes, der himmlischen Freuden, und der ewigen Seligkeit Erben eingesetzet. Mithin vergiß nicht, wie der Apostel Paulus, Coloßer 1, v. 12, 14. die Pflicht beschreibet. Saget Dank dem Vater der uns tüchtig gemacht hat, zum Erbtheil der Heiligen im Licht. u. s. w.

Die Taufzeugen waren Abraham Jost und Elisabetha Krämerin

Dieser Abraham ist gebohren und getauft in America, im Staat Pensylvanien in Bucks Caunty in Rakiel Taunschip

Confirmirt durch Hrn: Conrad Röller im Jahr. 1792.

Wenn wir kaum geboren werden, ist vom ersten Lebensstrit: bis ins kühle Grab der Erden, Nur ein kurz gemessener Schritt.
Ach mit jedem Augenblick! Gehet unsre Kraft zurück Und wir sind mit jedem Jahre,
allzu reiff zur Todtenbahre; Und wer weiß in welcher Stunde, uns die lezte Stimme weckt:
Dann GOtt hat's mit seinem Munde, Keinem Menschen noch endeckt.
Wer sein Haus nun wohl bestellt geht mit Freuden aus der Welt.
Da die Sicherheit hingegen; Ewigs Sterben kan erregen.

Ich bin getauft, ich steh im Bande,
Durch meine Tauf mit meinem Gott,
So sprech' ich stets mit frohem Munde,
In Creutz, in Trübsal, Angst und Noth,
Ich bin getauft, deß' freu ich mich,
Die Freude bleibet ewiglich.

READING:
Gedruckt
von Barten und Jungmann,
Im Jahr
1793.

Ich bin getauft, ob ich gleich sterbe,
Was schadet mir das kühle Grab?
Ich weiß mein Vaterland und Erbe,
Das ich bey Gott im Himmel hab,
Nach meinem Tod, ist mir bereit,
Des Himmels Freud, das Freuden-Kleid.

22. OPPOSITE. An unusual and beguiling Fraktur, printed by the firm of Barton & Jungmann, and decorated by the prolific Friedrich Krebs. He cut out the animal figures from a piece of embossed Dutch gilded paper, then colored them and pasted them onto the printed form. The floral motifs are hand-drawn. Probably Bucks County, Pennsylvania. 1793. 16⅛″ h. x 13⅛″ w. *(Franklin and Marshall College Collections)*

23. A Singbild (an illuminated hymn text), probably given to a student as an award. The eye is instantly drawn to the whimsical trumpeting angel, who tips the composition in an otherwise traditionally symmetrical drawing. Hand-drawn and colored on paper. Southeastern Pennsylvania. c. 1800. 7⅜″ h. x 6¾″ w. *(Barry Cohen Collection)*

24. Ink and watercolor bookplate made for Georg Schlott, rendering the patriotic eagle with the traditional motifs of flowers and arrows. Note the resemblance in fine detailing to the songplate on p. 25. Pennsylvania. First quarter of the 19th century. 5⅛″ h. x 3⅝″ w. (*Howard and Catherine Feldman Collection*)

25. OPPOSITE. A type of religious broadside called an "Irrgarten," related to medieval prototypes. The delicacy of the illustration and the strength of the overall labyrinthian design echo that of far more formal work in illuminated manuscripts. Dated 1824. Anonymous artist. Handdrawn and colored on paper. 12⅜″ l. x 12⅝″ w. (*Howard and Catherine Feldman Collection*)

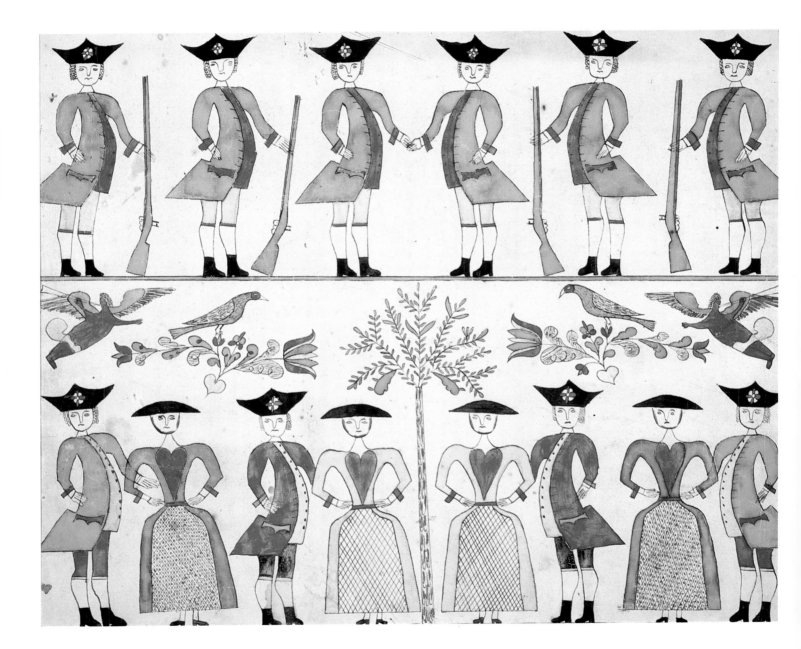

26. OPPOSITE. Fraktur drawing of what seems to be a military wedding. This watercolor and ink drawing by John Adam Eyer was probably a wedding present to one of his two brothers, both of whom served in the Revolutionary War. Note the hearts carried by the birds. Bucks County, Pennsylvania. 1790–1820. 15½″ h. x 12⅜″ w. (*Courtesy of the Henry Francis duPont Winterthur Museum, Winterthur, Delaware*)

27. Birth and baptismal certificate for Sara Seifer, 2 February 1826. The illustration and verse ("This heart of mine/Shall be but thine/O Jesus") have a cautionary quality—surely meant to encourage virtues such as piety and devotion. Artist unknown. 9⅛″ h. x 6¾″ w. (*Howard and Catherine Feldman*)

IV
TEXTILES

We learned to sew patchwork at school, while we were learning the alphabet;
and almost every girl, large or small, had a bed-quilt of her own begun, with
an eye to future house furnishing. I was not over fond of sewing, but I
thought it best to begin mine early.   —*Diary of Lucy Larcom,* 1889

APRIL 1. I wove two yards and three quarters and three inches to-day and I
think I did pretty well considering it was April Fool Day.
                                            —*Diary of Elizabeth Fuller,* 1791–92

THURSDAY A.M. (April 24)—All my scattering moments are taken up
with my needle.   —*Diary of Ellen Birdseye Wheaton,* 1851[1]

THE eighteenth- and nineteenth-century diaries of young girls and women record hours,
days, and months spent sewing thousands upon thousands of small stitches into the clothing and household furnishings of their families. Glorious appliquéd and pieced quilts,
embroidered samplers, hooked rugs, woven coverlets, cross-stitched rugs, embroidered show
towels and bedding testify to the inventive energy and artistic sensitivity of their makers.
     Preparation for a lifetime of sewing began young. Marion Nicholl Rawson recalls: "Before
I was three years old, I was started at piecing a quilt."[2] Young children of the emerging middle

28. OPPOSITE. Family record for Thomas R. and Elizabeth Plympton, stitched
by their eldest daughter, Louisa. Apparently the first Louisa died, and perhaps
also Fanny; their fruit is no longer attached to the tree. There are twelve
known samplers of this basic design in the Lexington-Concord area. Louisa
Plympton's is one of two stitched in the long oyster-white silk threads that
give the sampler its glistening quality. The Plympton family lived in Sudbury,
Massachusetts, and later moved to Waltham. 18″ l. x 16″ w. (*Collection of
Dorene Paoluccio*)

class were sent to dame schools. They then went on to academies, seminaries, boarding and day schools, or to public schools where the curriculum included crewel, plain sewing, fancy embroidery, and the making of a sampler to exhibit mastery of stitches. "Not a child was ever graduated from a school such as this who had not worked one sampler and more often two," wrote one woman in a memoir of girlhood.[3]

The first appearance of the heart motif on a sampler has been given as 1754.[4] By the late eighteenth century large and small hearts are found in samplers from many parts of the country, though rarely as a primary or central motif. The exquisite samplers from Miss Mary Balch's Academy in Providence, Rhode Island, often included an enchanting heart configuration: two flying angels suspended between paired birds perched on a chain encircling a heart-shaped locket (fig. 50). Other Balch school samplers contain the homily: "Teach us to number our days That we may apply our hearts to WISDOM."[5]

The time after school and before marriage was filled with hours of preparing the bed linens and quilt tops needed for setting up a new household. Once completed, these were neatly folded and put into dower chests and hope chests. In some communities young women were expected to complete thirteen quilt tops by the time they were married, the thirteenth, and finest, being the marriage quilt. This quilt was often embellished with appliquéd hearts (fig. 34). In some communities hearts were reserved for use only on bridal quilts. Another tradition held that the bride's quilt should be mostly white.[6] The exquisite white stuffed-work pillow sham, one of a pair, in (fig. 36), may have been made to accompany a bridal quilt.

On the pieced Amish quilts, restricted in design and color by the beliefs of this conservative sect, bridal hearts were stitched as part of the elaborate quilting on the borders or in the centers of these striking bed coverings.

Many sewing and weaving tools were adorned with a heart—gifts and love tokens given to the seamstress in appreciation of her contribution to the family. The wool winders and lap looms, used in weaving, were often inscribed and initialed, and many women wore a pair of "waistpockets" (often richly embroidered with hearts, flowers, berries, and vines) tied around the waist under the skirt.

29. Heart-in-hand grospoint change purse. Northern New England. c. 1840. 4″ x 4″. (Collection of Alan L. Daniel)

30. 19th-century heart pin-cushions on rope. Assembled by the owners. (*Collection of Nancy and Gary Stass*)

To a large extent, textiles were a copied art. Creativity was not encouraged. A letter in *Memories of Old Salem* points out: "[my sampler] was copied from an approved pattern, the teacher leading my fingers toward perfection."[7] An expertly copied design was more highly prized than the inferior execution of an original design. And yet every one was different, reflecting the eye of the maker, the skill of the hand, and the pride and personal care taken by each woman in her work. The design vocabulary of textiles was borrowed from cabinet-makers, Fraktur artists, and silversmiths. Lithographs, engravings in books, woodcuts, and magazines provided patterns; nature, friends, neighbors, teachers, political events, and popular culture inspired new variations.

Family records or genealogies were in fashion at the end of the eighteenth and through much of the nineteenth century. The schoolmaster and watercolorist William Saville of Gloucester, Massachusetts, used a family tree with inverted hearts at the base to create a popular design form. This same tree appears on a group of samplers from the Concord-Lexington area of Massachusetts. One of the most dazzling is the family tree of the Plympton family, done by Louisa H. Plympton (fig. 28). Instead of inverting hearts at the base of the tree, Louisa stitched intertwining hearts for her parents' names and marriage date, and framed them with another rainbow heart. Paired or intertwining hearts representing marriage were a common design in textiles, as were combinations of a heart with paired birds, and a single or double heart pierced by an arrow. These marriage motifs, appliquéd in presentation quilts and album quilts, were particularly popular in Baltimore, Maryland, between 1840 and 1850. The richly embellished squares that made up the so-called Baltimore Album quilts were filled with literal symbols from the lives and communities of the people for whom the quilts were made. Many also contain heart-shaped wreaths of vines or flowers (fig. 37B)—a motif found in Pennsylvania German quilts—signifying a blessing and protection of the home.[8] The Maryland quilters copied several motifs from their Pennsylvania neighbors, but it is hard to know whether the symbolic content was understood and shared, or whether the designs were adopted for purely decorative purposes. The heart wreath may have signified good fortune, as many quilts were given to honor a popular minister or teacher, to celebrate a wedding, or to bless the journey of departing friends.

The "heart and hand" is another recurrent motif in textiles, particularly quilts. In early eighteenth-century England, the heart and hand was used as a trade sign for marriage

31. Woolwinder, signed: "E. Frost." Connecticut. Late 18th century. 3′ h. (*Collection of Lillian Blankley Cogan*)

insurance offices, and its association with "giving one's hand in marriage" was continued in America. It was also associated with friendship, and later became one of the ritual emblems of the Independent Order of Odd Fellows, a benevolent fraternal organization active in America from 1819 into the twentieth century. Quilts made for members of the Odd Fellows and the Masons often contain the heart and hand or the heart and sword, along with other ritualistic symbols (fig. 8).

The heart on the "show towels" of southeastern Pennsylvania, popular from 1820 to 1850, echoes another Old World tradition. These long, narrow towels were embroidered or cross-stitched with typical Pennsylvania German motifs—stars, birds, flowers, tulips, and buildings (fig. 43). But in a study of more than six hundred towels, the most striking feature was found to be a heart with a crown above and vines sprouting from each side. Between the branches is the acronym OEHBDDE, composed of the first letters of the German phrase, *O Edles Herz Bedenk Dach Dein Ende* (O noble heart, reflect on thine end).[9] Like hearts on Fraktur, this motif expressed a reaffirmation of faith for those who knew its meaning. For others it was a copied pattern, used decoratively.

The textiles and sewing implements that have survived from the eighteenth century show us the amount of time, devotion, emotional energy, and artistic expression that women poured into this magnificent body of folk art. In answering the needs of their families, these women also expressed the feeling in their own hearts.

32. Detail from a cross-stitched rug. The design is a familiar one on Pennsylvania German show towels: a heart at the center and geometric branches and crown emanating from it. But here the artist has added an echoing reflection of the heart in lavender. The entire rug measures 41″ l. x 29″ w. Southeastern Pennsylvania. c. 1850–1900. (*Collection of Patricia and Donald Herr*)

33. OPPOSITE. Hannah Riddle of Woolrich, Maine, won first prize at the Woolrich Fair in 1870 for this appliqué coverlet, made of felt and bordered with strips of blue velvet. Here we find a windmill, a horse pull-toy, a house, a sailing ship, a cat, many flowers in their pots, and a number of other enchanting objects harder to identify. The kinship of form and color of the berries, clover leaves, and hearts reinforces the overall effect of a cherishing imagination. 77½″ l. x 76″ w. (*Harriet Griffin Fine Arts Inc. Photograph courtesy of E. P. Dutton*)

34. Center of a pieced and appliquéd marriage quilt, with buttonhole stitching around the hearts. New Jersey. c. 1825–50. (*Collection of Thos. K. Woodard*)

36. OPPOSITE. Stuffed-work pillow sham, one of a pair. Vines spring from the heart to form a wreath around it. c. 1800–50. 24″ l. x 17″ w. (*Collection of Gail van der Hoof and Jonathan Holstein*)

35. Scrimshaw bodkin, with inlaid polka dots and diamond scribe lines. The instrument was used both for making lace and for splicing strands of rope. c. 1870. 4″ h. (*Collection of Barbara Johnson*)

37A&B. Two squares from a Baltimore bride's quilt top. The intertwining hearts and bird represent a marriage, the wreathed heart a wish for good fortune. Signed: "Sarah A. Shafer." 1850. 107″ l. x 106″ w. *(Courtesy of America Hurrah Antiques, New York City)*

38. Hooked and shirred rug. Mid-19th century. 36″ l. x 21″ w. *(Collection of Barbara Johnson)*

39. In this needlepoint rug…hearts within hearts, an infinity of hearts. Southeastern Pennsylvania. 1850–1900. 52″ l. x 36″ w. *(Collection of Patricia and Donald Herr)*

40. Silk pincushion made with hand-wrought pins. In some communities, it was the tradition to hang a pillow on the front door to announce the arrival of a newborn baby, and they were often inscribed: "Welcome Little Stranger." New England. c. 1800–20. 4″ h. x 6½″ w. (*Collection of Nancy and Gary Stass*)

41. An exceptionally endearing quilt, made for a treasured doll, c. 1880. 18¼″ l. x 17″ w. (*Collection of Nancy and Gary Stass. Photograph courtesy of Thos. K. Woodard*)

42. Coverlet border design from a double-weave blue wool and white cotton coverlet. Woven by David D. Haring, Bergen County, New Jersey. 1833. *(Collection of Mr. and Mrs. Foster McCarl, Jr. Courtesy of Abby Aldrich Rockefeller Folk Art Center)*

43. Detail from a Pennsylvania show towel, cross-stitched on a plain-weave linen ground. A richly fanciful and geometric design by a girl who was a poetic seamstress but a careless speller! The entire towel measures 54″ l. x 16″ w. Pennsylvania. 1835. *(Collection of Patricia and Donald Herr)*

44. OPPOSITE. Eliza Ann Hunt's sampler includes the birth and marriage dates and, *in memoriam*, the dates of death of her mother and stepmother, both of whom died by the time she was nine years old. Silk on linen. 1824. 16½″ l. x 17¼″ w. *(Courtesy of Cooper-Hewitt Museum, The Smithsonian Institution's National Museum of Design, New York)*

45. A sampler of a similar pattern—Rebecca Wild's, dated 1831. Because of the large love knot in the intertwined hearts, the reversed heart—signifying the marriage—is slightly out of kilter. Charlestown, Massachusetts. 16½″ l. x 17¼″ w. *(Collection of Mary Jaene Edmonds)*

46. Peter Emman's sampler, dated 6 August 1836. Note the two small inverted hearts tucked into the upper corners of the rug that frames the heart. 9½″ l. x 7½″ w. (*Museum of American Folk Art*)

47. A rose wreath encircles the intertwined hearts and the crooked arrow in this silk-on-linen sampler. Note the paired birds on either side. Possibly New Hampshire. Dated 10 February 1832. 19¾″ l. x 16¾″ w. (*Courtesy of America Hurrah Antiques, New York*)

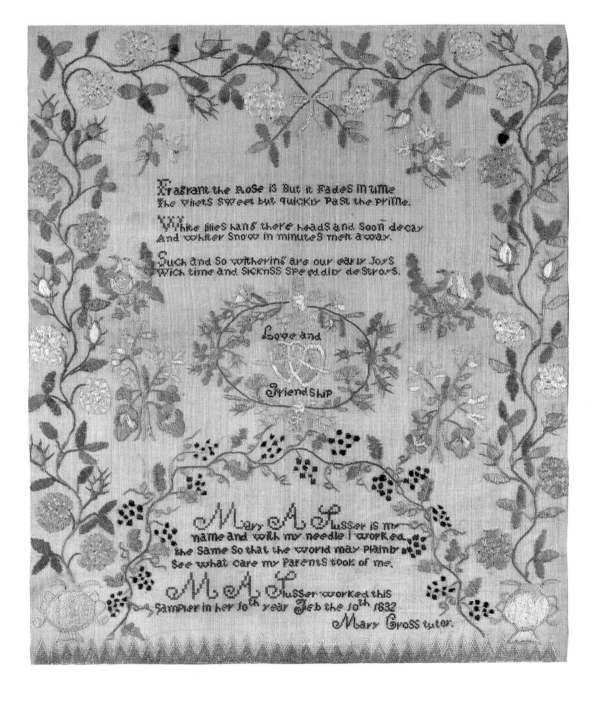

48. Child's embroidered linen pocket—one of a pair worn under the skirt for carrying sewing implements. The placement of the heart gives it the quality of a locket. And the flowers appear to be formed by joining four hearts. Hudson River Valley. Mid-18th century. 8¾″ l. x 6″ w. at center. (*Barry Cohen Collection*)

49. BELOW. Wool hearth rug, appliquéd and embroidered. A dazzling variation of heart shapes forming flowers (and, on the border, leaves). Ohio. Late 19th century. 66¾″ l. x 29½″ w. (*Collection of Helaine and Burton Feldman*)

50. OPPOSITE. Lydia Gladdings' sampler, October 1796. The pupils of the Balch school in Providence, Rhode Island, made samplers renowned for their design and execution. Here there are five animals, three birds, two couples, and two trumpeting angels. Love reigns over all. 12″ x 12″. (*Courtesy of Robert Bishop*)

May hypolets innocence & truth my every action guide and guard my unexperiencd youth from arrogance and pride

LYDIA GLADDINGS WORK PROVIDENCE October 1796

51. Maple armchair. Connecticut. c. 1770. 36″ h. (*Collection of Susan and Robert E. Klein*)

52. "Heart and crown" armchair, possibly made by Nathaniel Street of the Norwalk area in Connecticut. This style of American country chair is considered the most highly developed and visually exciting. 1725–45. 48⅞″ h. (*Collection of Lillian Blankley Cogan*)

53. "York" side chair. Maker unknown. Connecticut. 1790–1820. 40″ h. (*Collection of Robert and Cynthia Schaffner*)

V

COUNTRY FURNISHINGS

AT its best, country furniture is one of the most visually exciting expressions of American ingenuity and innovation. Outside the major port cities and style centers, rural carpenters and joiners met the economic limitations, utilitarian needs, and simple tastes of their communities by creating functional furniture from native woods. Much of this furniture was enlivened by an imaginative and exuberant use of paint or simple abstract carving and incising. The heart as an element of the design vocabulary of these country craftsmen appears on the chests, chairs, beds, and tables that filled country homes.

As early as the last quarter of the seventeenth century, hearts appear on the English-inspired scratch-carved "Sunflower" or "Hadley" chests of the Connecticut River Valley. The entire surface of these chests was embellished with tulips, leaves, pinwheels, and hearts, then painted or stained. By the end of the seventeenth century simplified versions of these chests were produced, with uniquely polychrome painted motifs replacing the more elaborate scratch carving (fig. 68). The geometric, compass-drawn decorative features of this Hadley-type chest of drawers include an inverted heart in the center of each drawer front. On the polychrome chests, as Dean Fales and Robert Bishop point out in their book *American Painted Furniture 1660–1880*, "paint had replaced carving, and inventiveness and expediency joined together to produce an effect which, though outdated, was one of true resplendence."[1] While the earlier carved Hadley chests copied English motifs, the inverted heart, compass-drawn motifs, and polychrome paint combined to create an American design innovation.

The heart made another significant appearance along the Connecticut coastline, incised in the crest rail of what have become known as "heart and crown" chairs in the Norwalk, Stratford, Guilford, and Milford communities. Early inventories label them "crown chairs," presumably because of the crownlike effect created by the crest rail. Thomas Salomon (1693–1749), a turner and a highly skilled carpenter and joiner, is credited with making the first known examples in the early 1720s.[2] An inventory of 1789 notes "six old crown back and great chairs," valued far below the earlier inventories, signifying a decline in their popularity by the last quarter of the eighteenth century.[3]

54. Small initialed 18th-century mirror. Farmington, Connecticut. 7½″ h. *(Collection of Lillian Blankley Cogan)*

It is interesting to study the variations and configurations of these immensely appealing chairs from the superb examples gathered here. Compared to the four-heart crest (fig. 52), the molded hearts with two elongated hearts create a more "folksy" effect (p. viii). The heart turns up again in splats on country chairs by the joiner John Durand of Bedford, New Hampshire (fig. 62), and it appears again in "York" chairs as other rural Connecticut carpenters adopted the popular heart motif in the early nineteenth century (fig. 53).

The communities of southeastern Pennsylvania, where immigrants from Germany, Switzerland, and Alsace settled, employed the bold heart motif in abundance in their painted furniture. Following Old World customs, the Pennsylvania Germans were expected to provide a dowry for their daughters. Dower chests were made by local joiners, and given as gifts to young girls by their parents. Itinerant artists, often Fraktur painters, transmitted their designs onto these chests. Others were painted by amateurs copying traditional motifs. The broad, compass-delineated, flattish heart, more horizontal than vertical, found its boldest expression in the large flat surfaces of dower chests. As a central motif it might enclose the inscribed name of the owner and a date (fig. 71).

Pieces from the various counties and communities throughout southeastern Pennsylvania possessed their own distinctive regional characteristics. The Schwaben Creek Valley in Northumberland County developed highly stylized motifs, which were applied freehand and with stencils on brightly painted backgrounds. In this closely knit community, craftsmen painted delicate Fraktur-inspired flowers, birds, hearts, vines, stars, deer, angels, leaping rabbits, and horses onto locally made chests, chests of drawers, desks, and cupboards from 1798 to 1834.

The chest of drawers in fig. 57 is a superb example of Schwaben Creek Valley furniture. The hand-painted birds perched on flower branches, the vines spiraling from a heart painted the depth of the top three drawers, and the design base on the bottom drawer are typical of all the painted pieces dating from 1827 to 1834. Dresser drawers began to supersede the traditional dower chests during the 1820s and early 1830s as Pennsylvania Germans adopted this more convenient form from their English neighbors, adding their own characteristic motifs. Like dower chests, many dresser drawers have the owner's name and a date, and were used to store linens and quilts in preparation for marriage.[4]

The Pennsylvania grain-painted bedstead (fig. 72), with its broad, flattened heart on the headboard, evokes the splendid grace and movement achieved by this type of painting popular in the first half of the nineteenth century. Pennsylvania German dowry books note that typical gifts were "cooking utensils, house linens, a bed and a cow."[5] This bed would have made a treasured wedding gift, as the heart is a glorious artistic and emotional statement.

Even country homes would have appeared empty without either pictures or mirrors on the walls. The demand for a personal likeness was again met by itinerant artists, who traveled from town to town painting portraits in oil, watercolors, or cut-paper silhouettes. While hearts are rarely found in the marvelous galaxy of folk portraiture, they occasionally appear on the clothing of sitters. The fireman in the portrait by a member of the group of William Matthew Prior (fig. 70) wears gaily decorated suspenders sporting a bright red heart, perhaps a symbol of courage for the proud firefighter. A small heart locket on the beguiling silhouette water-color of a young girl, proudly worn for her portrait, was probably a gift from a parent or other relative. Heart lockets were a favored gift for young girls. On January 4, 1772, Anna Green Winslow writes of getting all dressed up and wearing her heart locket:

> I was dressed in my yellow coat, my black bib & apron, my pompedor shoes, the cap my aunt Storer sometime since presented me with (blue ribbons on it) & a very handsome locket in the shape of a heart she gave me....[6]

Paper cuttings were another popular art form found in country homes. The best of these were framed and hung. Using different types of paper, a nimble cutter would fold the paper in half, trace a scene then deftly cut the traced design. A dazzling example of cut paper is the

55. An exceptionally delicate chip-carved tramp-art mirror. Late 19th century. 16½″ diameter
(Collection of Helaine and Burton Fendelman)

gold-foil paper cutting or mourning picture by an anonymous Pennsylvanian, hand-cut around 1850 (fig. 73). The heart surrounds the mourner and tombstone, a familiar device used to emphasize the enclosure, and perhaps here to express everlasting love and affection for the deceased.

Looking glasses were very rare and costly; until 1800, most country homes had only one. They would be smaller and less ornate than the high-style urban mirrors of master craftsmen, but the two frames in figs. 54 and 61, each crowned with hearts, have the appealing and treasured quality of love tokens.

Watercolor and ink family records or genealogies were another popular art form executed by a member of the family, an itinerant artist, or the local schoolmaster during the last quarter of the eighteenth and first half of the nineteenth century. A number of these artists incorporated hearts as an integral part of their basic design—among them, the two New England artists, J. Pool and William Saville of Gloucester, Massachusetts (figs. 66 and 67). William Murray, who worked along the Mohawk Valley in New York, used bold red and black hearts to frame the names and birth dates of family members (fig. 3).

From the Maine–Vermont–New Hampshire border areas, family records drawn by the now renowned "heart and hand" artist were composed of a simple list of names and dates in columns, embellished with hearts and hands drawn in the scalloped and draped borders framing the genealogies. Hearts also surround the wedding date. On rare occasions this artist signed his work in mirror image (fig. 64). Although difficult to decipher precisely, the signature appears to be "Samuel Lawhead" or "Samuel Lawhend." The "heart and hand" artist also executed trade cards or calling cards with his familiar rebus, as seen in fig. 13.

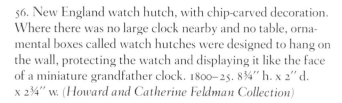

56. New England watch hutch, with chip-carved decoration. Where there was no large clock nearby and no table, ornamental boxes called watch hutches were designed to hang on the wall, protecting the watch and displaying it like the face of a miniature grandfather clock. 1800–25. 8¾" h. x 2" d. x 2¾" w. (*Howard and Catherine Feldman Collection*)

57. Schwaben Creek Valley four-drawer dresser, masterfully painted with Fraktur-inspired motifs. Dated 1836. 52″ h. x 42″ w. *(Private Collection)*

58. Watercolor portrait in miniature, with "hollow-cut" (un-painted) face. This anonymous artist also painted companion portraits of the subject's mother, father, and elder sister. Probably New England. c. 1835. 4½″ l. x 3½″ w. *(Collection of Robert Bishop. Photograph courtesy of E. P. Dutton)*

59. Pennsylvania German foot stool. Polychromed wood. 14″ l. x 8″ h. *(Private Collection)*

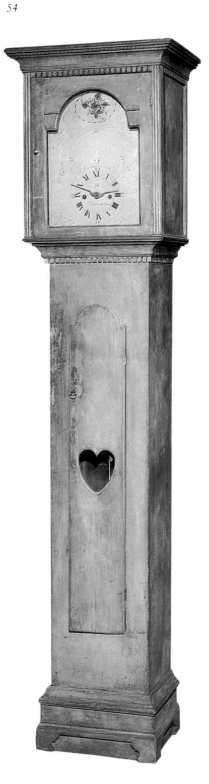

61. Mid-18th-century mirror, carved and painted pine. Probably New England. 20″ h. x 9⅜″ w. (*Courtesy of Museum of American Folk Art*)

62. Maple side chair, attributed to Major John Dunlap (1746–92) of Bedford, New Hampshire. Painted dark blue-green. 45″ h. x 21¾″ w. (*Courtesy of the Henry Francis duPont Winterthur Museum, Winterthur, Delaware*)

60. Tall case clock, painted buttermilk blue. Made by John Edwards of Ashby, Massachusetts. c. 1810. 18½′ h. (*Courtesy of George E. Schoellkopf. Photograph courtesy of E. P. Dutton*)

63. Painted and decorated
storage box. Pennsylvania.
12″ l. x 7¾″ w. *(Collection of
Lillian and Jerry Grossman)*

64. Many family records were made by itinerant painters. This one was
drawn by the now celebrated "heart and hand" artist, who worked in Maine,
Vermont, and New Hampshire from 1830 to 1856, and who signed this piece
in an elusive manner occasionally employed by such artists. By holding
a mirror up to the record, one can make out the name "Samuel Lawhead"
(or "Lawhend"). The entry of the date of death of the baby Mary Hodgdon
appears to be the last in his hand. Dated 21 November 1830. 12½″ l. x
10½″ w. *(Collection of Nancy and Gary Stass)*

65. Carved and incised pine
blanket chest, with scrolled
hearts. New England. 1713.
42½″ l. x 17″ d. x 19¾″ h.
(Private Collection)

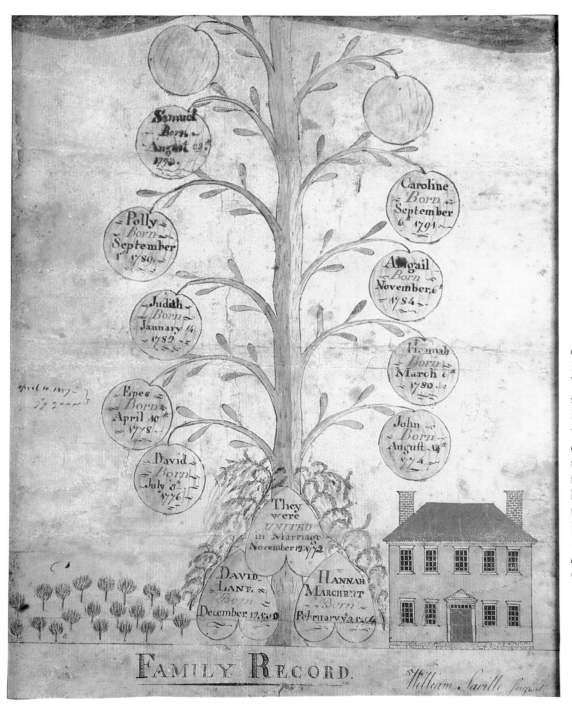

66. David Lane–Hannah Marchent family record by William Saville, who was a schoolmaster in Gloucester, Massachusetts, as well as a watercolor artist. The drawing emphasizes the classical architecture of the house. The configuration of the overlapping hearts gives them an almost three-dimensional quality. Dated 21 December 1772. 11½″ h. x 9¼″ w. (*Howard and Catherine Feldman Collection*)

67. Olive Clark–Andrew Bickford family record, signed by J. Pool, who took pains to create a faithful and charming record of their house and farm as well. Watercolor. New England. 19th century. 15″ l. x 12″ w. (*Private Collection*)

68. Oak chest of drawers with polychrome decoration. The painted geometric patterns echo earlier carved designs. From the Hadley area of Massachusetts. 1675–1720. 46¼″ h. x 20¾″ d. x 43½ w. (*Courtesy of the Henry Francis duPont Winterthur Museum, Winterthur, Delaware*)

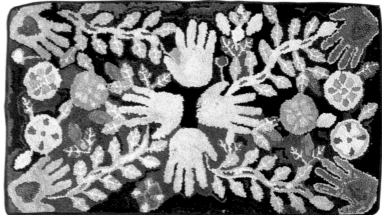

69. Hooked rug, c. 1875. Here, the vines linking the hands create a lyrical pattern with a mosaic effect. The hands in the center once had hearts, too. New Jersey. 38″ l. x 22″ w. (*Courtesy of America Hurrah Antiques, New York City*)

70. Oil painting of a fireman attributed to the group of William Matthew Prior. 36″ l. x 29″ w. Probably Boston. c. 1840. Fire companies such as the Heart and Hand Company of New York City in the late 18th century frequently used the heart as an emblem on their hats, buckets, or suspenders. *(Courtesy of the New York State Historical Association, Cooperstown, New York)*

71. Several of the Pennsylvania German motifs on this painted pine chest are handled in unusual ways—most particularly the birds in the heart, who do not face each other, and the trout-like fish with their folkloric simplicity in an otherwise highly geometric composition. The chest is inscribed with the name Cadarina Rexin (Catharina Rex) of Northampton (Lehigh) County, and the date, 1780. 21¾″ h. *(Collection of Richard S. and Rosemarie B. Machmer)*

72. Pencil post bedstead, made of
poplar and grain-painted in orange
and dark brown. Pennsylvania.
1790–1810. 7′1″ h. x 6′2¾″ l.
(*Philadelphia Musem of Art, Titus
C. Geesey Collection*)

73. Gold-foil cut-paper mourning picture by an unknown artist. Note the pairs of birds throughout—especially those perched atop the tombstones, rendered in the Egyptian style that was gaining popularity in the folk art of this period. And don't miss the squirrels. Pennsylvania. c. 1850. 16″ h. x 20″ w. (*Collection of Robert Bishop*)

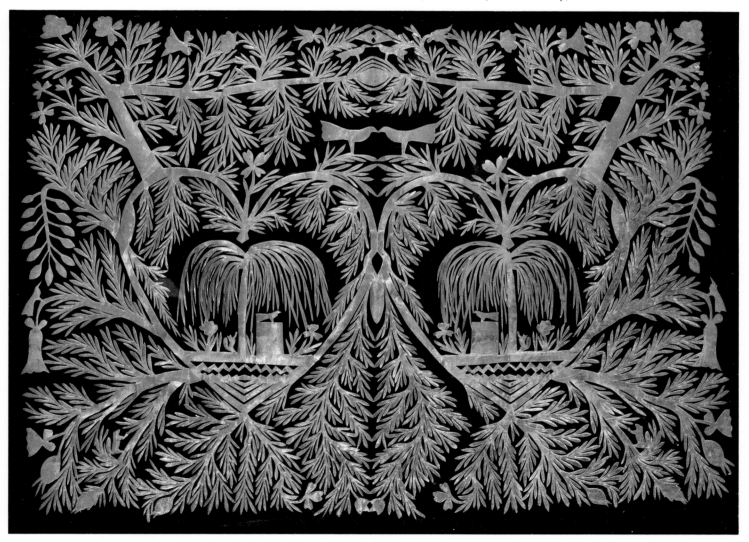

74. Pine knife box. 19th century.
10″ l. (*Private Collection*)

75. Painted shoe-polish box.
Schuykill County, Pennsylvania. 1800–30. 17″ l. (*Philadelphia Museum of Art, Titus C. Geesey Collection*)

76. Wide splint basket, decorated with vegetable paint.
New England. Late 19th century. 10″ h. x 8″ sq. (*Collection of Helaine and Burton Fendelman*)

VI

BOXES

Box. 1. Case made of wood or other matter to hold anything. It is distinguished from a chest as the less from the greater.

> —*Samuel Johnson's*
> *Dictionary of the English Language,*
> *1775 edition*

D R. JOHNSON'S wonderfully concise definition of a box testifies to the ubiquitous
nature of the boxes that filled early country homes. A box and its contents were often
the only material possessions brought to America by the earliest settlers, and these trans-
ported boxes were often put to use as furniture. "Bible boxes" were the forerunner of dresser
drawers, and slope-lid desk boxes later became the prototype for desks-on-frames and slant-
front desks.

The primary purpose of boxes was for storage, thus aiding in the organization of home and
workplace. As Nina Fletcher Little summarizes in her book on boxes, *Neat and Tidy*:

> For general convenience, personal use, domestic purposes, and special needs
> boxes have always proved indispensable, because despite lack of drawer
> space, dearth of closets, and crowded rooms they enabled those who so
> desired to keep their household possessions neat and tidy.[1]

Old boxes were made from materials at hand—wood, tin, whalebone, cardboard, and papier-
mâché—and came in every size and shape. Most were used for storing a myriad of household
items: linens, clothes, sewing materials, games, butter, cheese, herbs, writing equipment,
money, documents, jewelry, pipes, salt, candles, and trinkets, plus a variety of now obsolete

77. 18th-century pine box—possibly for dominoes. 15″ l. x 4½″ h. *(Private Collection)*

items. Expertly constructed by carpenters, hand-crafted or later factory-made, the broad, flat sides of boxes provided superb surfaces for decoration. The earliest boxes and chests displayed chip carving echoing the designs on European boxes and chests. Eastern Connecticut chip-carved boxes often included a heart, star, and pinwheel, common motifs borrowed from Old World medieval iconography.

By the beginning of the nineteenth century the use, variety, and decoration of boxes increased to meet the new needs and tastes of an expanding population. Country arts and folk art flourished. Itinerant artists and amateurs alike decorated utilitarian boxes with the same exuberance, vitality, and flair they brought to furniture. Grain painting, stenciling, and representational hand-painted scenes embellished box surfaces in waves of popularity during the first three quarters of the nineteenth century.

Many boxes were simple and expendable; others were treasured and became heirlooms. Boxes that were dated and initialed or bore the name of the owner often documented important events in their owners' lives—particularly weddings. The document box belonging to Johanna Klinger dated 1827 (fig. 63) is typical of many boxes bearing the bold compass-delineated Pennsylvania German heart, framing Fraktur-style script. In southeastern Pennsylvania it is believed that Fraktur artists also decorated boxes, dower chests, and furniture, which explains consistency of designs and styles.

78. Painted vanity box, inscribed: "CD 1754," with looking glass inside. The hole at the top allows for hanging. Connecticut. 3½″ l. x 2½″ w. *(Collection of Lillian Blankley Cogan)*

A box made by a country craftsman might be joined, then personalized and painted by the maker, as seen in the early Connecticut pipe box (fig. 83). The two outlined and chiseled hearts—one for the date, 1723, and the other for the initials, B.B.—were further emphasized by a coat of red paint, traces of which remain today.

The cleverly composed heart on a hand-painted split-ash covered basket (fig. 76) is also initialed by the artist, on the bottom. Hearts so elaborately conceived testify to their intended message as a gift of love or friendship. The extra care and effort taken by the folk artist, the ability to put something of himself into a heart, is what makes this motif so endearing.

The little hand-whittled and -carved heart-shaped boxes are among the most compelling of all, enchanting us with their unmistakable intimacy (fig. 81). Careful examination reveals something of the maker and the receiver in each of these love tokens, which fit into the palm of your hand. There are secondary hearts, initials, and dates; traces of leftover snuff; and inside one a small chip of mirror on the top and hollowed space for powder on the bottom.

79. 18th-century tinderbox with
two carved hearts. Connecticut. 8″ l.
(Collection of Lillian Blank ey Cogan)

The efforts of sailors in scrimshaw often express a similar intimacy between maker and receiver. The ditty box (fig. 82), with its intricately incised heart, speaks of many hours of toil and longing.

A hand-painted shoe-polish box from Pennsylvania (fig. 75) tells another kind of tale of matrimony. The central motif on the top features a proud prancing horse, surrounded by a radiating star, a pair of birds, and polka-dotted circles, stars, and hearts. Painted inside the top is a pair of tamed and bridled (and bridalled) horses, their reins tied to a central post.

Just as the heart form is often used to frame script, it is also common to find heart-shaped key plates or escutcheons surrounding the keyholes of boxes. A sealskin sailor's box (fig. 85) gives expression to the notion of "unlocking the heart." The heart and key association suggests something of the box's contents—probably love letters, diaries, or other personal keepsakes. The need to keep money and documents in locked boxes is a less romantic but equally plausible possibility.

Other boxes extol the beauty of the simple heart shape. Bandboxes, popular in the second quarter of the nineteenth century, were used for holding and transporting hats, bonnets, and wearing apparel. Heart-shaped bandboxes carried the "theater caps" of fashionable women to an evening at the opera or theater. The high bonnets worn to the theater were removed and replaced by a smaller cornet cap, which had been brought in the heart-shaped bandbox.[2]

Boxes made in the shape of books were popular during this same period, and the bold black hearts, red circles, and diamonds on a yellow ground of the Pennsylvania box in fig. 86 represent a glorious play of shape against shape, color against color.

Anyone who has ever opened such lovingly ornamented boxes, stored away in attics by generations past, senses with excitement the discovery that neatly packed boxes hold, particularly when filled with keepsakes of the heart.

80. Heart-shaped miniature bandbox, used for keepsakes and trinkets. New England. 1800–25. 4″ l. x 2½″ h. x 4¼″ w. *(Barry Cohen Collection)*

81. Miniature heart-shaped boxes, hand-whittled and -carved. From the left, counter-clockwise: vanity box, snuffbox, molded heart box from Massachusetts probably made for a ring or precious locket, and heart-shaped box with looking glass. All 18th century. *(Collection of Lillian Blankley Cogan)*

83. This pipe box was originally painted black, and the hearts and Connecticut-style roses red. Inscribed: "BB 1723." 12½" h. x 6¾" w. (*Collection of Lillian Blankley Cogan*)

84. A more formal pipe box, with the kind of decorative styling associated with mirrors and chairs. The drawers were used for flint and tobacco. Connecticut. 18th century. 20½" h. x 3¾" d. x 10" w. (*Collection of Lillian Blankley Cogan*)

82. Small whalebone ditty box. Perhaps the house on top was the sailor's own. c. 1835. 10¼" l. x 3¾" w. (*Collection of Barbara Johnson*)

85. Sealskin-covered box, with heart-shaped key plate. The sealskin is framed and fastened with strips of whalebone. c. 1830. 6¼" h. x 9¾" w. (*Collection of Barbara Johnson*)

86. Book-shaped box, painted
wood. Pennsylvania. c. 1835.
5½″ l. (*Private Collection*)

87. Tramp-art hanging wall
pocket, polychromed wood.
Possibly Pennsylvania.
1875–1900. 18⅛″ h. x 8⅛″ w.
(*Private Collection. Photograph courtesy of E. P. Dutton*)

88. Scrimshaw "jagging wheel" or pie crimper of whale ivory and whalebone. Nantucket. c. 1850. 6″ l. (*Collection of Barbara Johnson*)

89. Cottage cheese mold, typically in the shape of a heart. These were also used to make pressed egg cheese at Easter, a favorite of the Pennsylvania Germans. Pierced tin. 18th century. 6″ h. x 5″ w. (*Private Collection*)

VII
HEARTS IN THE KITCHEN

The kitchen, the place where the family really lived, was a spacious room, with a large fireplace toward the front and low windows at the back. Here over the open fire the cooking was done. The bread was baked in the brick oven built into the chimney; the meat was roasted on the spit that was kept turning in front of the glowing coals. The floor was covered with white sea sand, swept into patterns by a homemade broom. In the center of the room was a long table and around it were wooden chairs painted yellow. A big armchair stood by the fireplace, and bright pewter platters and blue china dishes stood on a big dresser in the corner.

Beside the fireplace was a heavy wooden cradle, in which all the babies of the family in their turn were rocked to sleep. In the big fireplace was a little seat or settle where the children could creep on wintry nights and by the hickory-log blaze read in the Children's Primer until Mother lighted the candle and packed them off to the cold trundle bed in the next room.

In Old Southampton[1]

ATTITUDES, personal taste and styles were reflected in the utilitarian objects that hung on beams, were displayed on shelves, and placed near the large fireplace in country kitchens. Many of these kitchen utensils had a heart wrought, carved, or incised into the patterns that embellished them. In some cases these were purely decorative devices; in others the heart was featured as a symbol of love and pride. Potters, farmers, ironmongers, tinsmiths, and other craftsmen created useful objects imbued with a strong decorative quality to enliven the kitchen and add another dimension to this simple, practical room.

During and after the Revolution, most kitchen articles were made from wood, clay, or iron. Craftsmen applied their carving and whittling skills to the production of dishes, trenchers, butter molds, and simple bowls. The burl bowl in fig. 90 is a fine example of woodenware made for everyday use but with a high level of artistic quality. It was probably a love token for a New England housewife, with its delicate cut-out heart handles and refined shape. The wooden spoon, (fig. 94), with a simple heart incised on the handle, is reminiscent of the Welsh spoons that were popular love tokens for one's sweetheart. Wooden pieces were used along with simple utilitarian pottery and some pewter.

China was not common in country homes, though some families had a few prized pieces. John M. Newton from Marlboro, Vermont, described his tableware in 1815:

91. Wrought-iron trivet. Probably New England. Early 19th century. 7¾" l. x 5" w. (*Collection of Nancy and Gary Stass*)

> Everything was of the simplest and plainest style, with one exception— my mother had a China tea set.... [People] ordinarily ate from wooden trenchers, and on such occasions as Thanksgiving and Marriage feasts, from pewter platters burnished bright as silver, which had been handed down from one generation to another....[2]

90. Burl bowl. Connecticut or New York. c. 1710. 11½" l. x 4½" d. x 9½" w. (*Collection of Lillian Blankley Cogan*)

Craftsmen expressed their love for decoration by carving fanciful designs in pine, poplar, maple, or fruitwood. Wooden butter prints were chip-carved with simple, bold designs. In southeastern Pennsylvania the familiar motifs seen on furniture, textiles, and Frakturs were also carved on butter molds, and the tulip, star, and heart were repeated as an important decorative motif on Pennsylvania butter molds (fig. 97).

Stoneware was made for storing items in the kitchen, dairy, cellar, or pantry. Because of its durability and lack of porosity, salt-glazed stoneware proved practical and sturdy. Jugs and crocks, jars and bottles, were used to store liquids, pickled vegetables, butter, and salted meats. The gray or tan clay containers, when fired at high temperatures, became hard and dense. A salt-glaze was applied during firing to make them even less porous. The small earthenware pitcher (fig. 96), was made at the first Moravian community in Broad Bay, Maine. But slip-decorated earthenware was not as practical as salt-glazed stoneware because of its porous nature.

Pies were a staple food in American homes. The fruit pie was the most common, for berries grew in great abundance. The pie crimper or pie-crust cutter was a standard utensil in every kitchen. Memories of home-baked pies often invoked the creative impulse, and sailors aboard whaling ships made exquisite pie crimpers of whale bone and whale ivory (figs. 88

92. Whalebone pie crimper. Note the heart-shaped handle with the teeth for piercing the crust. This little masterpiece contains at least a baker's dozen of hearts. 6″ l. (*Collection of Barbara Johnson*)

and 92). These love tokens are among the most dazzling and endearing of all scrimshaw pieces.

A bride's dowry included many kitchen utensils that were decorated with the symbol of love and marriage—the heart. It was customary in Pennsylvania German families for the parents to give their daughter for her dowry a fork, spatula, and taster, each decorated with a heart. Wedding gifts with a heart emblem were popular and commonly signified the union of marriage. A Connecticut woman mentions in her diary the utilitarian wedding presents that expressed friendship:

> November 2, 1785—I have written one more date in this perfectly kept journal, for yesterday was my wedding day, and we came immediately to this house which is henceforth to be my home. May our Heavenly Father bless us in this new life! A good many of the young people came here with us, most of them bringing some little useful article with their expression of kindness and goodwill.[3]

On special occasions such as Easter and Christmas, baking was a central part of the festivities. As one diarist wrote:

> It was the week before Christmas. A busy week in the country home, for then "the butchering" had to be done. The second day before Christmas the cooky-baking was done. Large tables in the bake house were covered with cookies, in all manner of forms—birds, horses, hearts, lambs, stars, all carefully spread out on Patty Pans….[4]

Tin cookie cutters with the heart and hand and the simple heart mold were used mainly at Christmas and Easter by the Pennsylvania Germans, and strung together and hung in the attic when not in use.

Country kitchens served as the heart of the home. The objects that filled this room reflect an extra warmth that comes from constant use—they comfort, soothe, and rekindle memories.

93. Maple sugar mold, with the graceful curve at the tail characteristic of northern New England. 19th century. 14¾″ l. x 4″ w. (*Collection of Susan and Robert E. Klein*)

94. Wooden spoon with
heart and tree design.
New England. 18th cen-
tury. 8½" l. (Collection
of Lillian Blankley
Cogan)

95. Wood and tin grater,
used for horseradish.
19th century. 11¼" l. x
1½" w. (Collection of
Lillian and Jerry
Grossman)

96. Redware pitcher,
with yellow slip decora-
tion, from one of the
first Moravian commu-
nities in Broad Bay,
Maine. Dated 1756.
8½" h. (Barry Cohen
Collection)

97. Butter molds for
stamping butter. c. 1800–50.
3½" w x 6½" h.
(Private Collection)

98. Kitchen utensils decorated with hearts were traditional gifts to newlywed daughters. Wrought iron and brass. Northumberland County, Pennsylvania. Inscribed 1832. Each 19½″ l. *Spatula and fork (Collection of C. Keyser Stahl), taster (Collection of Hilda Smith Kline)*

99. Wrought-iron two-tined roasting fork. c. 1700–1800. 15¾″ l. *(Philadelphia Museum of Art, Collection of Titus C. Geesey)*

101. Unpainted wooden cookie cutter, banded by tin. Probably Pennsylvania. c. 1800–50. 2⅞″ h. x 15/16″ d. x 3⅛″ w. *(Henry Francis duPont Winterthur Museum, Winterthur, Delaware)*

100. Five-hearted waffle iron. Pennsylvania. c. 1800–50. 14¾″ in diameter. *(Philadelphia Museum of Art: Gift of J. Stogdell Stokes)*

102. Salt-glazed stoneware crock, probably used for butter or lard. c. 1825–50. 13″ h. x 13½″ w. (*Private Collection*)

103. All-wood foot warmer. A heated brick wrapped in flannel was placed in it. Made for "D.K." in 1810. Pennsylvania. 10″ l. x 7½″ d. x 6″ w. (*Collection of Lillian and Jerry Grossman*)

104. Salt-glazed stoneware water or cider cooler. 16″ h. x 40″ around. Made by Van Wickle and Morgan Potters in Herbertsville, New Jersey. c. 1823–38. (*Barry Cohen Collection*)

105. Front and back of brass cookie cutter. Pennsylvania. c. 1840. 3½″ l. x 2½″ w. *(Barry Cohen Collection)*

106–109. Four cookie cutters, showing a variety of ways in which tinsmiths rendered heart and hand imagery. 19th century. *(Collection of David P. and Susan M. Cunningham)*

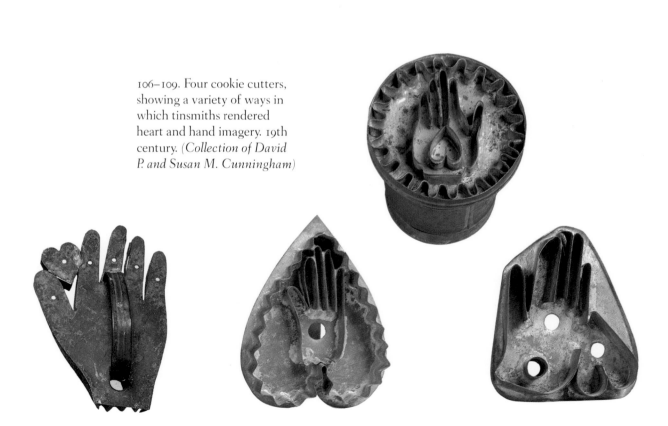

110. Slate tombstone of Dr. John Dunsmoor, dated 1747. He survived his own children by two years. Lancaster, Massachusetts. 29″ h. (Photograph courtesy of Daniel and Jessie Lie Farber)

VIII
HEARTS IN SCULPTURE

O N gravestones, weather vanes, and other folk sculpture, the heart was proudly carved, etched, or incised by our ancestors in America. Borrowing from European traditional styles and customs, but also creating his own design motifs, the folk carver expressed his feelings concerning love and friendship, death and resurrection, through the symbol of the heart.

Gravestones in New England form the earliest dated American folk sculpture. Against the background of a preoccupation with death, the Puritans expressed both their fears and their hopes of rebirth through salvation and resurrection. As Peter Benes points out:

> Although some of this interest was an inheritance from Elizabethan and Jacobean England, New England's engagement with death was derived principally from the region's Puritan religion. Eheoretically, death represented a welcome opportunity to end a dangerous worldly pilgrimage during which an individual might at any time learn he had been predestined to damnation. A Puritan who could look forward with some assurance to his salvation perceived death in terms of its opposite (everlasting life) and anticipated the experience with an emotion he might at least pretend was joy. To the extent that he could not, however, he continually reminded himself of the subject in order to stimulate his search for this assurance. In this respect, death and religion enjoyed a mutually supported relationship, each stimulating and gaining impetus from the other.[1]

Symbolic messages interpreting religious beliefs about death were carved on rural gravestones. An after-life spirit in the shape of a winged skull or face was often carved on the upper portion of the gravestone, signifying the anticipated resurrection.[2] To this face, secondary

symbols were added, such as the heart. Fig. 11 shows a heart-shaped face with a mouth in the shape of another heart—a symbol of love, affection, and eternal life.[3] In fig. 120, the winged skull form is shown with the heart boldly carved at the top. Here the effigy figure is portrayed on its journey toward eternal life. In fig. 110 the heart contains the vital information of the deceased and expresses the abiding love and affection of those left behind. With little formal training in carving and a limited knowledge of sculptural expression, farmers, housewrights, surveyors, and others who carved tombstones created symbols of everlasting love and the continuance of life after death.

The early American weather vanes were also created by local folk carvers and amateurs whose backgrounds influenced the objects they made. Vanes of iron, copper, or wood were proudly displayed on homes, churches, barns, and meetinghouses to indicate wind direction. Most hand-made vanes were wrought by the local blacksmith, carpenter, or farmer in his spare time, either for himself or for a neighbor.

The English brought with them the memory of banner-style weather vanes. In fig. 112, the gracefulness of the swallow-tailed banner is further enhanced by a bold cut-out heart. Another cut-out heart and whimsical bird forms a creative combination on the scroll-bodied weather vane in fig. 114. The scroll form descended from the banner style; it is believed that minor additions such as the shore bird were added during the latter part of the nineteenth century.

After the Revolution, a patriotic fervor enveloped America. This was evidenced by three major decorative emblems—the eagle, Uncle Sam, and the angel Gabriel—symbolizing the newfound democracy. Gabriel became the American envoy who proclaimed the newfound freedom.[4] In fig. 122, the heart in conjunction with the angel Gabriel might have suggested an emblem of love for the new democracy.

A heart carved on the palm of the hand symbolized the friendship of an "unselfish giver whose hand is always extended to a brother."[5] Heart-and-hand carvings were used in the ceremonies and rituals connected with the secretive Independent Order of Odd Fellows, a fraternity that originally attracted members from the middle and industrial classes, offering them sick and death benefits in times of distress. During a candidate's initiation he was asked to practice friendship, love, and truth, represented by the three links of Odd Fellow signs. In fig. 113, these links are combined with a red heart. The heart with a hand was used as the official emblem of the order. This symbol reminded the members:

....that whatsoever the hand finds to do, the heart should go forth in unison, and render the tasks doubly sweet by its savor of affection. The Lord loves a cheerful giver. The work entrusted to us to perform should be one of love, pursued from the promptings of the heart and altogether freed from the taint of mercenary or selfish motives.[6]

Friendship and feelings of affection arise from the heart, guiding our hands in all good works.

112. Swallow-tail banner weather vane. Wood and metal, painted yellow. New England, probably Massachusetts. Late 18th century. 35″ l. x 8¾″ w. (*Barry Cohen Collection*)

111. OPPOSITE. This was the official emblem of the Independent Order of Odd Fellows. It was a tenet of theirs that "whatsoever the hand finds to do, the heart should go forth in unison, and render the tasks doubly sweet by its savor of affection." Perhaps there is added significance to the way the thumb holds the heart in place. Gilded and polychromed wood. Found in Pennsylvania. 10½″ h. (*Collection of Alan L. Daniel*)

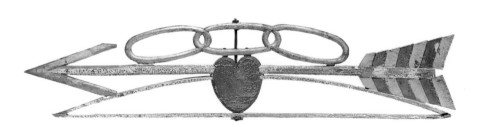

113. An Odd Fellows' meeting house sign with the three links symbolizing friendship, love, and truth. Painted wood. Eastern United States. Late 19th century. 3′1″ l. x 8¼″ w. (*Private Collection*)

114. Scroll weather vane, thought to be from the
S. S. Pierce mansion in Boston, Massachusetts.
The bird may have been a later addition. Wood,
tin, and iron. c. 1850. 48″ l. x 32″ w. (*Private
Collection*)

118. OPPOSITE. Tombstone
portrait of Patience Watson,
dated 1767. Slate. Plymouth,
Massachusetts. 33″ h. (*Photograph courtesy of Daniel and
Jessie Lie Farber*)

115. A particularly graceful late 19th-century
heart-in-hand hatchet with the traditional Odd
Fellows' symbolism of linked chains and heart in
hand. Polychromed wood and tin. Diagonal
measurement: 26¼″ l.; blade 14″ l. (*Collection
of Alan L. Daniel*)

116. Andirons with
patterned hearts.
New England or
New York. c. 1840.
10½″ h. (*Collection
of Alan L. Daniel*)

117. Wrought-iron
child's stirrup. New Eng-
land. Early 19th century.
4″ h. x 3″ w. (*Collection
of Alan L. Daniel*)

119. Tombstone of Daniel
Outman, dated 1803. White
marble stone. Arlington, Vermont. 38″ h. *(Photograph
courtesy of Daniel and
Jessie Lie Farber)*

121. Tombstone with motif typically seen on
Pennsylvania German Frakturs: the tree of life
with the tulip growing from the heart. Dated
1753, the year of the marriage of F. C. and Martin Herbster. Emanuelsville Church Cemetery,
Emanuelsville, Northampton County, Pennsylvania. *(Courtesy of the Pennsylvania German
Society: Guy Reinert Collection, Photograph by
Guy Reinert)*

120. Tombstone of William Til-
ley, dated 1717. The bold heart at
center is echoed in the shape of
the skull and in the overall design
of the wings framing the skull,
meant to assist the flight of the
departed soul. Possibly carved by
Nathaniel Emmes of Boston,
Massachusetts. Slate. 15″ h.
*(Photograph courtesy of Daniel
and Jessie Lie Farber)*

122. Mid-19th-century weather vane. New York. 24⅝″ l. (*Howard and Catherine Feldman Collection*)

123. Swordfish weather vane. Found in Pennsylvania. Early 19th century. 32″ l. (*New York State Historical Association, Cooperstown, New York*)

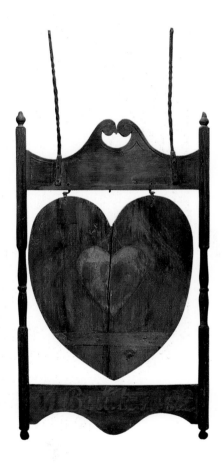

124. Painted wood tavern sign from New Hampshire. A star is carved on the reverse, suggesting that the tavern was known as "The Heart and Star." Dated 1802. 48″ l. x 27¼″ w. (*Courtesy of America Hurrah Antiques, New York City*)

125.
Pennsylvania
German cut-work
love letter, with
hearts, angels, and
crowns. Four hearts
form a star at the center.
Decorated by a Fraktur artist.
Dated 27 May 1754. 12½″ diameter.
(*Private Collection*)

IX
HEARTS IN LOVE LETTERS, VALENTINES, AND LOVE TOKENS

1. My Dearest Dear and blest devine
   I've pictur'd here your heart on mine
   A heart my Dear I present to you
   A heart that is sincere and true

2. But cupid with his cruel dart
   Has deeply pierc'd my tender heart
   A heart that ne'er will incline to join
   To any other heart but thine

3. And hath between us set a cross
   Which make me to lament my loss
   This I my Dear have sent to thee
   To show how firm my love should be

4. But I'm in hopes when that is gone
   That both our hearts will be in one
   Grant me thy love my dearest Dear
   And ease my heart of all its cares.

—Puzzle Purse Love Letter,
c. 1790–1810

 THE longings of the heart found glorious expression in the lovingly embellished, hand-decorated love letters, valentines, and love tokens of the late eighteenth and early nineteenth century. Depicted in pen-and-ink and watercolors, cut with scissors, or outlined

with pinpricks, these sentimental tokens of affection were given throughout the year, not just on February 14, St. Valentine's Day. Before the uniform postal service was established in America, love letters were hand-delivered, either left on the doorstep or hung on the front door. By the 1850s printed valentines, sent on February 14 to sweethearts, friends, and relatives, established St. Valentine's Day as it is now celebrated.

Before the Civil War, St. Valentine's Day celebrations evoked courting customs and romantic traditions from England and Germany. Until the nineteenth century a Valentine meant a person, not a card or love letter, and St. Valentine's Day traditions centered on various methods of choosing a Valentine or sweetheart. One English tradition, continued in New England, held that the first lad a young girl saw in the morning who was not a member of her family was her Valentine.[1] Anna Green Winslow's diary of 1771 refers with little enthusiasm to this custom:

> Valentine Day. My cousin Sally reeled off a 10 knot skane of yarn today. My valentine was an old country plow-jober. The yarn was of my spinning.[2]

Not a terribly eventful day, and certainly Anna Winslow seems quite underwhelmed by her Valentine.

Another English custom brought to America was the drawing of one's valentine by lottery on the eve of St. Valentine's Day. Samuel Pepys' famous diary notes this custom in an entry dated February 16, 1667: "I find that Mrs. Pierce's little girl is my valentine, she having drawn me...."[3] The verse on the American cut-work valentine in fig. 144, dated 1815, alludes to the same custom:

> This thirteenth day of February   It was my lot for me to be merry   It was my fortune and my lot to draw your name out of a hat   When lots were cast and I you drew kind fortune says it must be you....

The genuine exuberance of this message suggests the possible rigging of lotteries to assure that a special name was drawn.

The custom of giving hand-decorated love letters replete with hearts and lovingly written verse was introduced in America by the Pennsylvania Germans around 1750. The Liebesbrief, or love letter, an outgrowth of the Fraktur tradition, was given throughout the year and

126. Tenth anniversary gift, made of tin. Found in Connecticut. 1830–50. 11¼″ l. (*Collection of Nancy and Gary Stass*)

127. Pierced-tin sander, used to blot ink, and given as a love token. Connecticut. 18th century. Top, 3″ in diameter; 2¾″ h. (*Collection of Lillian Blankley Cogan*)

took several forms—true lover's knots, pinpricks, cut-work, and puzzle purses. If sent on February 14, they were considered valentines, otherwise the broader term love letter applied.[4]

The most common of these forms were circular-shaped, cut-work love letters, created by folding a piece of paper and then skillfully scissor-cutting a design on the folded edge. When unfolded, the repeated patterns created a lacelike effect. Some cut-work love letters were left plain; others were filled with tender thoughts written in minute penmanship, as in fig. 143.

Adam Dambach of Lancaster, Pennsylvania, inscribed his burning love in each of twenty hearts, set in a field of vines and flowers (fig. 137). The verses are in German, but one English translation reads: "My heart, which burns out of love's passion, would like to know what hers does."[5] Each verse is numbered, 1 through 20, and yet arranged in a slightly random fashion to elicit the close attention of Adam's sweetheart.

The true lover's knots—a continuous labyrinth forming intertwining hearts—were introduced during the first decade of the nineteenth century. An amorous inscription wound through the tunnels, and the reader had continually to turn the paper as she read her special verse. Daniel Stall's true lover's knot, in fig. 136, was carefully decorated with pen and ink and watercolor, the verses written in English instead of German. Love letters were considered personal communications and would have been carefully tucked away out of sight, put into a box or a chest.

Puzzle purses or fold-up love letters were decorated on both sides of the paper, then each corner was folded one inside the other to form an envelope. Upon opening, each section revealed a loving verse until the inside appeared, containing a small reward. The puzzle purse pictured in fig. 148 is completely open, revealing the last message written above the enchanting young man picking a heart from a tulip tree. Donald A. Shelley, in his definitive book *The Fraktur-Writings or Illuminated Manuscripts of the Pennsylvania Germans,* maintains that this type of love letter was the culmination of its predecessors "as regards intricacy of plan, artistry of execution, and amount of decoration—for it is completely decorated on both sides of the paper!"[6]

Early valentines and love letters were also found outside Pennsylvania. The heart and hand, a recurring motif in folk art in the nineteenth century, provided an immensely appealing design in the love token in fig. 142. The romantic notion implicit in this configuration is found on the inscription of one of the hands: "Hand and heart shall never part. When this you see remember me." One seventeenth-

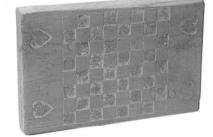

128. Miniature checkerboard, inscribed: "RA 1784." Connecticut. 7½″ l. x 4¾″ w. (*Collection of Lillian Blankley Cogan*

century English St. Valentine's Day custom was the giving of a gift of gloves, often accompanied by the verse:

> If that from Glove, you take the letter G
> Then Glove is Love and that I send to thee.[7]

Such a gift was a favored form of marriage proposal. If a young lady accepted, she wore her gloves to church on Easter Sunday.[8]

Small, intricately designed hearts, hearts and hands, or hearts and keys, without verse, were often created by young girls and boys to be given as tokens of love and esteem to friends and teachers on St. Valentine's Day and throughout the year. These tokens, seen in figs. 141 and 145, show painstaking efforts and are strikingly graphic and beguiling. Cupid's arrow piercing the heart was another configuration that grew in popularity just after the turn of the century. Its appearance was a bit puzzling to Catherine Elizabeth Havens, who at age thirteen wrote in her diary on April 15, 1850:

> When I grow up I think I shall have a beau, and his name is Sam B. and he lives across the street, for he sent me a valentine he painted himself, and it is a big red heart with an arrow stuck through it, and one of my school friends says that means he is very fond of me, but I don't see much sense in the arrow.[9]

129. Wooden bootjack. It is believed that this was made by the bride's father as a gift to the groom. Connecticut. 18th century. 15″ h. (*Collection of Lillian Blankley Cogan*)

130. 17th-century redware inkwell with yellow-glaze decorative dots. Cheshire area, Connecticut. 4½″ l. (*Collection of Lillian Blankley Cogan*)

Holidays and anniversaries, weddings and birthdays, provided further opportunities for the giving of love tokens. Often gifts such as presentation plates and salt-glazed stoneware were specially commissioned from potters and contained a heart. The stoneware flask in fig. 10 was initialed and presented by a thoughtful friend in 1860. The oversized tin locket and chain in fig. 126 could have been a tenth wedding anniversary gift; too large to be worn, it became a treasured love token.

While the Shakers, a religious sect that practiced austerity and simplicity, would not have made valentines, there does exist a small group of hand-painted, heart-shaped gifts which were presented to honored and faithful members of the community. Included in the heart-shaped gifts were simple messages and small illustrations, which were themselves part of the design vocabulary of the Christian-Shaker community, used in their spiritual drawings (fig. 151).[10]

Whether on love letters, valentines, or love tokens, the heart symbolized true feeling, the most treasured and sacred of human emotions.

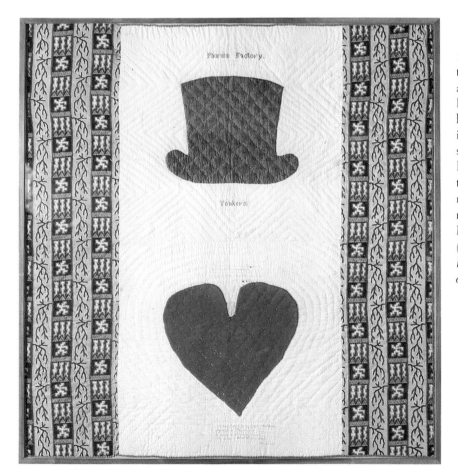

131. A folk art classic. A valentine in the form of a crib quilt, appliquéd with chintz borders. Inscribed above and below the heart (with minor variations in the wording): "A Heart I send you Squire Baldwine/ Reject it not I do implore thee/A warm reception may it meet/My name a secret I must keep" [Signed] "Old Maid." c. 1850. 34½″ l. x 32½″ w. (*Collection of Linda and Irwin Berman, Photograph courtesy of Thos. K. Woodard*)

132. Whalebone busk, inserted in the corset to widen the cleavage and support posture. c. 1840. 12¼″ h. (*Collection of Barbara Johnson*)

133. Portrait of a lady engraved on a sperm whale's tooth. c. 1835. 7½″ h. (*Collection of Barbara Johnson*)

134. "Sailor's Valentines" were popular from the early 19th century up to the 1880s. This one, c. 1860, was made of shells pasted on newspaper and framed in wood. Typically hinged in the style of a locket. Nantucket. 12″ l. x 9¼″ w. (*Collection of Barbara Johnson*)

135. Hand-thrown stoneware ink-well and sander, with five quill holes incised with floral and stamp decoration and embellished with cobalt blue slip. The name "Tyler" appears on the bottom. Made by William Crolius of New York City and dated 1773. 4¾″ h. x 5¾″ w. *(Barry Cohen Collection)*

136. Daniel Stalls drew this traditional German token of affection. "A True Lover's Knot" (incorporating the older German form of a labyrinth) for Mary Finkenbiner. As if to make it official, an eagle and the Pennsylvania state seal appear above the lover's knot. Ink and watercolor on paper. Probably Cumberland County, Pennsylvania. 1824. 13⅜″ l. x 8″ w. *(Courtesy of Rock Ford–Kauffman Museum, Lancaster, Pennsylvania)*

138. Oval red earthenware platter, with slip and sgraffito decoration. Pennsylvania. c. 1825–30. 14½″ l. x 9¾″ w. (*Private Collection*)

137. OPPOSITE. Cut-work love letter from Adam Dambach, inscribed with a multitude of endearments. These were often folded and intended to be read section by section. They were not meant for display and were never framed or hung in the home. Watercolor and ink. Lancaster, Pennsylvania. 1779. 12⅜″ l. x 12⅝″ w. (*Courtesy of the Henry Francis duPont Winterthur Museum, Winterthur, Delaware*)

139. Earthenware plate with slip decoration and clear lead glaze. Made by George Huebner for Cadarina Raederin, and inscribed: "Out of earth with understanding the potter makes everything." Dated 1786. Upper Hanover Township, Montgomery County, Pennsylvania. 12½″ diameter. (*Philadelphia Museum of Art: Gift of John T. Morris*)

140. A red earthenware sugar or tobacco jar, with slip and sgraffito decoration, dated 1822. Southeastern Pennsylvania. 10″ h. (*Howard and Catherine Feldman Collection*)

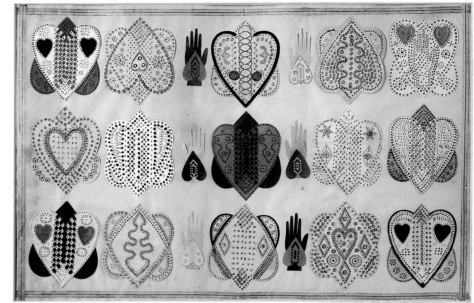

141. Cut-out and applied watercolor
love token, with thirty large reversed
hearts. Small hearts abound
throughout. It's fun to count them.
Probably New England. c. 1820.
11½″ h. x 16″ w. *(Private Collection)*

142. Heart-and-hand love token. Pen
and ink on cut paper mounted on
tissue on a card, and inscribed
"Heart and hand shall never part/
When this you see remember me."
Probably Connecticut. c. 1850. 14⅛″
h. x 12″ w. *(Museum of American
Folk Art)*

143. OPPOSITE. Cut-work valentine
with quite a lot of exclamation!
Pennsylvania. c. 1790. 9⅛″ l. x 9⅛″ w.
*(Hallmark Historical Collection,
Hallmark Card, Inc.)*

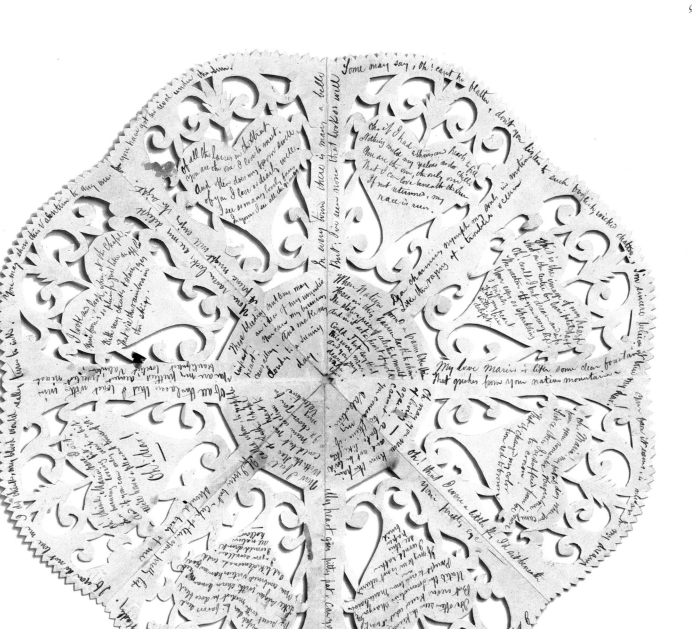

144. Cut-work valentine signifying a tender courtship. Dated 1875 and inscribed: "This thirteenth day of February It was my lot to be merry. It was my fortune and my lot to draw your name out of the hat." Pennsylvania. 13″ diameter. (*Barry Cohen Collection*)

145. Love token, handmade with knotted strands of hair. Possibly Connecticut. c. 1810. 2½″ l. x 2¼″ w. (*Hallmark Historical Collection, Hallmark Card, Inc.*)

146. Nine hearts make this hooked rug a fine valentine. c. 1885. 36½″ l. x 28½″ w. *(Collection of America Hurrah Antiques, New York City)*

147. 19th-century cut-work love token. The cut-out was mounted on another piece of paper, then the hearts and other decorative elements were filled in with colored ink. Pennsylvania. 6½″ diameter. *(Collection of Riki and Eugene Zuriff)*

As turns the needle to the pole
So my fond heart's inclin'd
To the bright magnet of my soul
And you my Valentine!

148. OPPOSITE. Watercolor puzzle purse, given as a love token and folded in triangles to form a puzzle square. When it is opened, a picture of a man picking a heart from a tulip tree is revealed. The challenge is to fold it up again and piece the heart on top together. Pennsylvania. c. 1790–1810. 12½″ square. *(Barry Cohen Collection)*

Two details from the reverse side of this Pennsylvania watercolor puzzle purse.

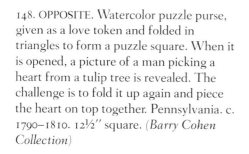

149. Cut-work love letter, hand-drawn and colored by Christian Strenge, bearing sixteen messages from his heart, among them: "My dearest one, I can no longer keep the feelings of my heart from you," and, "In my thoughts I have often kissed you, because you are such a pretty maiden." Lancaster County, Pennsylvania. c. 1800. 12½″ diameter. (*Courtesy of the Henry Francis duPont Winterthur Museum, Winterthur, Delaware*)

150. OPPOSITE. This water-color on paper was probably a school exercise in calligraphy. Pennsylvania. 19th century. 5½″ diameter. (*Private Collection*)

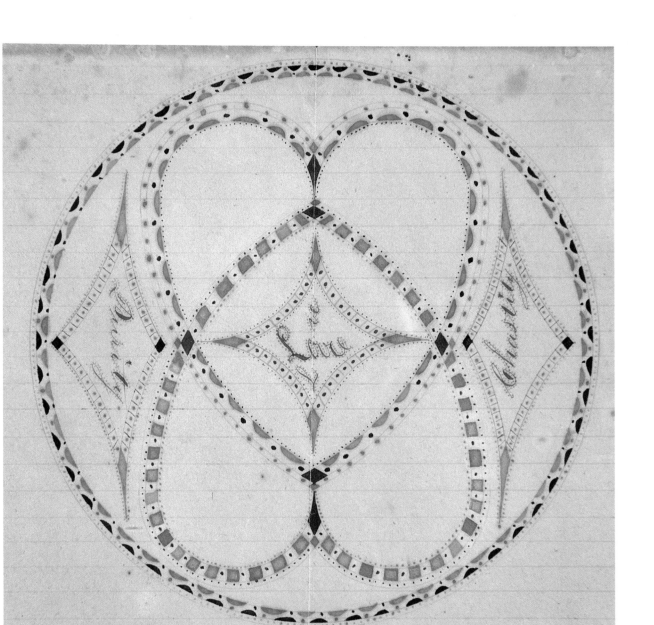

151. Shaker heart-shaped reward, given on 21
April 1844, to Rufus Bishop, who was appointed
to the ministry by Mother Lucy Wright and became one of the most respected of the early
Shakers. "Hands to work and hearts to God" was
the Shaker motto. Watercolor and ink. (*Courtesy
of Hancock Shaker Village*)

Notes

I. Introduction

1. Quoted in Glee Krueger, *New England Samplers to 1840* (Sturbridge, Mass.: Old Sturbridge, Inc., 1978), pp. 12 and 13.

II. Heart History

1. Donald A. Mackenzie, *The Migration of Symbols and Their Relation to Beliefs and Customs* (New York: Alfred A. Knopf, 1926), p. 67.

2. Robert Thomas Rundle Clark, *Myth and Symbol in Ancient Egypt* (London: Thames and Hudson, 1959), p. 62.

3. Elaine Eff, "Folk Art: The Heart of America," *The Clarion* (Summer 1978), p. 18.

4. *The Book of the Dead, Facsimile of the "Papyrus" of Ani in the British Museum* (London: Harris & Sons, 1980), plate 3.

5. *Das Herz Als Motiv in der Volkskultur.* Exhibition Catalogue, Gemeinsame Sonderausslellung des Etnografski Muzej Zagreb und des Burgenlandischen Landesmuseums (Eisenstadt, 1983), p. 13.

6. *The Secular Spirit: Life and Art at the End of the Middle Ages.* Exhibition Catalogue, The Metropolitan Museum of Art (New York: E. P. Dutton, 1975), p. 215.

7. R. Brasch, *How Did It Begin?* (New York: David McKay, 1966).

8. H. S. Hansen, *European Folk Art in Europe and the Americas* (New York: McGraw-Hill, 1968).

9. Reinhard Peesch, *The Ornament in European Folk Art* (New York: Alpine Fine Arts Collection, Ltd., 1983), p. 109.

10. Frans Unterkircher (ed.), *King Rene's Book of Love (Le Cueur d'amours éspris)* (New York: George Braziller, 1980).

11. Peesch, p. 109.

12. The other scenes of courtship in the box include a woman combing her lover's hair; two lovers embracing; the couple reclining; the man holding a flower toward the lady; and the lady giving her girdle to her lover. Inside the box is a relief of the Seated Virgin and Child.

This is a wonderful transitional example of the heart symbol from religious love to secular love.

13. Peesch, p. 110.

14. Samuel Johnson, *A Dictionary of the English Language,* Vol. I (Dublin: Thomas Ewing, 1775).

III. Hearts on Fraktur

1. Frederick S. Weiser, "From the Cradle to the Grave: Something about Pennsylvania German Personal Documents and Folk Art," *Pfalzer-Palatines* (1981), pp. 375, 376.

2. Frederick S. Weiser, "Piety and Protocol in Folk Art: Pennsylvania German Fraktur Birth and Baptismal Certificates," *Winterthur Portfolio,* Vol. 8 (1973), p. 43.

3. Our heartfelt thanks to Frederick S. Weiser in sharing information on this Fraktur.

4. Weiser, "Piety and Protocol," p. 35: "Moreover, the fact that a high percentage of those preparing Taufscheine were rural, parochial Lutheran and Reformed schoolmasters, who also taught the fourth r of religion (and who were usually parish organists and choirmasters), suggests the more strongly that the documents, at least initially, were intended to be part of the structure of a person's religious belief."

IV. Textiles

1. All three diaries quoted in Mirra Bank, *Anonymous Was a Woman* (New York: St. Martin's Press, 1979), pp. 20, 22, and 92.

2. Marion Nicholl Rawson, *When Antiques Were Young* (New York: E. P. Dutton, 1931), p. 129.

3. Mary H. Northend, *Memories of Old Salem: Drawn from the Letters of a Great-Grandmother* (New York: Moffatt, Yard & Co., 1917), p. 111.

4. Ethel Stanwood Bolton and Eva Johnston Coe, *American Samplers* (New York: Dover Publications, 1973), p. 28.

5. Krueger, *New England Samplers to 1840*, p. 24.

6. Patsy and Myron Orlofsky, *Quilts in America* (New York: McGraw-Hill, 1974), p. 49.

7. Northend, *Memories of Old Salem*, p. 105.

8. Orlofsky, *Quilts in America*, p. 260.

9. Ellen Gehret, "Oh Noble Heart...An examination of a motif of design from Pennsylvania embroidered hand towels," *Der Regge-bage, Quarterly of the Pennsylvania German Society*, Vol. 14, no. 3 (July 1980), pp. 1–15.

V. COUNTRY FURNISHINGS

1. Dean A. Fales, Jr., and Robert Bishop, *American Painted Furniture 1660–1880* (New York: E. P. Dutton, 1979), p. 20.

2. Robert F. Trent, *Hearts & Crowns* (New Haven: New Haven Colony Historical Society, 1977), p. 39.

3. Benno M. Forman, "The Crown and York Chairs of Coastal Connecticut and the Work of the Durands of Melford," The Magazine *Antiques*, Vol. CV, no. 5 (May 1974), p. 1148.

4. Frederick S. Weiser and Mary Hammond Sullivan, "Decorated Furniture of the Schwaben Creek Valley," *Ebbes fer Alle-Ebber Ebbes fer Dich, Something for Everyone—Something for You, Essays in Memoriam Albert Franklin Buffington*, by Albert F. Buffington, *et al.* (Breingsville, Pa.: The Pennsylvania German Society, 1980), pp. 333, 336, 354; and Frederick S. Weiser and Mary Hammond Sullivan, "Decorated Furniture of the Mahantango Valley," The Magazine *Antiques*, Vol. CIII, no. 5 (May 1973), pp. 932–933.

5. Jeanette Lasansky, "Unusual Pennsylvania Ironware," The Magazine *Antiques*, Vol. CXIX, no. 2 (February 1981), p. 439.

6. Alice Morse Earle, ed., *Diary of Anna Green Winslow, A Boston School Girl of 1771.* (Boston: Houghton Mifflin, 1894; reprint, Williamstown, Mass.: Corner House Publications, 1974), p. 13.

VI. BOXES

1. Nina Fletcher Little, *Neat and Tidy: Boxes and Their Contents Used in Early American Households* (New York: E. P. Dutton, 1980), p. xviii.

2. Lillian Baker Carlisle, *Hat Boxes and Bandboxes at The Shelburne Museum*, Museum Pamphlet Series #4. (Shelburne, Vt.: The Shelburne Museum, 1960), pp. 91–92.

VII. HEARTS IN THE KITCHEN

1. Abigail Fithian Halsey, *In Old Southampton* (New York: Columbia University Press, 1940), p. 69.

2. Catherine Fennelly, editor, *Food, Drink, and Recipes of Early New England* (Meriden, Conn.: The Meriden Gravure Co., 1963), p. 10.

3. Ellen Strong Bartlett, "Bits from Great-Grandmother's Journal," *Connecticut Magazine*, Vol. 1, no. 3 (July, August–September 1895), p. 270.

4. Benjamin Mausman, "An Old-Time Christmas in a Country Home," *The Guardian* (January 1871), quoted in Jeanette Lasansky, *To Cut, Piece and Solder: The Work of the Rural Pennsylvania Tinsmith 1778–1908.* (Lewisburg, Pa.: The Oral Traditions Project of the Union County Historical Society, 1982), p. 56.

VIII. HEARTS IN SCULPTURE

1. Peter Benes, *The Masks of Orthodoxy* (Amherst, Mass.: University of Massachusetts Press, 1977), pp. 33–34.

2. *Ibid.*, p. 43.

3. *Ibid.*, p. 92. Peter Benes discusses the heart-shaped mouth in the work of the eighteenth-century tombstone carver, Nathaniel Fuller, from Plymouth County, Mass., suggesting that it may have been used "...to soften the 'heartless' quality of the child's ghost symbol."

4. Myrna Kaye, *Yankee Weathervanes* (New York: E. P. Dutton, 1975), p. 67.

5. Eff, "Folk Art: The Heart of America," p. 21.

6. Theodore A. Ross, *Odd Fellowship: Its History and Manual* (New York: The M. W. Hazen Co., 1888), pp. 575, 577.

IX. HEARTS IN LOVE LETTERS, VALENTINES, AND LOVE TOKENS

1. Frank Staff, *The Valentine and Its Origins* (New York: Frederick A. Praeger, 1969), p. 20.

2. Earle, ed., *Diary of Anna Green Winslow*, p. 25.

3. Staff, *The Valentine and Its Origins*, p. 21.

4. Donald A. Shelley, *The Fraktur-Writings or Illuminated Manuscripts of the Pennsylvania Germans* (Allentown, Pa.: The Pennsylvania German Folklore Society, 1961), Vol. 23, p. 52.

5. Beatrice B. Garvan and Charles F. Hummel, *The Pennsylvania Germans: A Celebration of Their Arts 1683–1850.* Exhibition Catalogue, The Philadelphia Museum of Art and The Henry Francis duPont Winterthur Museum, 1982, p. 157.

6. Shelley, *The Fraktur-Writings*, p. 54.

7. Edna Barth, *Hearts, Cupids and Red Roses: The Story of the Valentine Symbols* (Boston: Houghton Mifflin Co., 1974), p. 35.

8. *Ibid.*

9. Diary of Catherine Elizabeth Havens, as quoted in Bank, *Anonymous Was a Woman*, p. 48.

10. *The Gift of Inspiration: Shaker and American Folk Art.* Exhibition Catalogue, Hirschl & Adler Galleries, Inc., 1979, New York, p. 13.

Selected Readings

Adams, Ruth. *Pennsylvania Dutch Art*. Cleveland: World Publishing Company, 1950.

Ames, Kenneth L. *Beyond Necessity: Art in the Folk Tradition*. Winterthur, Del.: The Henry Francis duPont Winterthur Museum, 1977.

Andrews, Charles M. *Colonial Folkways: A Chronicle of American Life in the Reign of the Georges*. New Haven, Conn.: Yale University Press, 1920.

Andrews, Ruth, ed. *How to Know American Folk Art*. New York: E. P. Dutton, 1977.

Ayres, James. *British Folk Art*. London: Barrie & Jenkins, 1977.

Bank, Mirra. *Anonymous Was a Woman*. New York: St. Martin's Press, 1979.

Barber, Edwin Atlee. *Pottery and Porcelain of the United States*. New York: Century House Americana, 1971.

———. *Tulipware of the Pennsylvania German Potters*. Philadelphia: The Pennsylvania Museum and School of Industrial Art, 1903.

Barth, Edna. *Hearts, Cupids, and Red Roses*. Boston: Houghton Mifflin, 1974.

Bartlett, Ellen Strong. "Bits from Great-Grandmother's Journal," *The Connecticut Magazine*, Vol. 1 (July, August, and September 1895), p. 270.

Bayer, Walter E. "The Meaning of Human Figures in Pennsylvania Dutch Folk Art," *Pennsylvania Folklife* (Fall 1960), pp. 5–23.

Bishop, Robert. *The American Chair 1640–1970*. New York: E. P. Dutton, 1972.

———. *American Folk Art: Expressions of a New Spirit* (Exhibition Catalogue). New York: Museum of American Folk Art, 1982.

———. *Folk Painters of America*. New York: E. P. Dutton, 1979.

———. *Folk Sculpture*. New York: E. P. Dutton, 1974.

Bolton, Ethel Standwood, and Eva Johnston Coe. *American Samplers*. New York: Dover Publications, 1973.

Bornman, Henry S. *Pennsylvania German Bookplates*. Philadelphia: Pennsylvania German Society, 1953.

Bowne, Eliza Southgate. *A Girl's Life Eighty Years Ago: Selections from the Letters of Eliza Southgate Bowne*. Introduction by Clarence Cook. New York: Charles Scribner's Sons, 1887.

Brant, Sandra, and Elissa Cullman. *Small Folk: A Celebration of Childhood in America*. New York: E. P. Dutton, 1980.

Brasch, R. *How Did It Begin?* New York: David McKay, 1965.

Burwell, Latitia M. *A Girl's Life in Virginia Before the War*. Philadelphia: Frederick A. Stokes Company, 1895.

Carlisle, Lillian Baker, *Hat Boxes and Bandboxes at Shelburne Museum* (Museum Pamphlet Series No. 4). Shelburne, Vt.: The Shelburne Museum, 1960.

———. *Pieced Work and Appliqué Quilts at Shelburne Museum*. (Museum Pamphlet Series No. 2). Shelburne, Vt.: The Shelburne Museum, 1957.

Chase, Ernest Dudley. *The Romance of Greeting Cards*. Cambridge, Mass.: University Press, 1927.

Christensen, Edwin O. *The Index of American Design*. Washington, D.C.: National Gallery of Art, 1950.

Cooper, Wendy A. *In Praise of America*. New York: Alfred A. Knopf, 1980.

Crawford, Mary Caroline. *Social Life in Old New England*. Boston: Little, Brown, 1914.

Crosby, Everett U. *Susan's Teeth and Much About Scrimshaw*. Nantucket, Mass.: Tetaukimmo Press, 1955.

Dow, George Francis. *Everyday Life in the Massachusetts Bay Colony*. New York: Benjamin Bloom, 1935.

Duval, Frances Y., and Ivan B. Rigby. *Early American Gravestone Art in Photographs*. New York: Dover Publications, 1978.

Earle, Alice Morse. *Customs and Fashions in Old New England.* Rutland, Vt.: Charles E. Tuttle, 1973.

————, ed. *Diary of Anna Green Winslow: a Boston School Girl of 1771.* Boston: Houghton Mifflin, 1894. Reprinted Williamstown, Mass.: Corner House Publishers, 1974.

Eff, Elaine. "Folk Art: The Heart of America," *The Clarion Magazine* (Summer 1978), pp. 17–35.

Emery, Sarah Anne. *Reminiscences of a Newburyport Nonagenarian.* Bowie, Md.: Heritage Books, Inc. Reprint of the 1879 edition issued by W. H. Huse under the title: *Reminiscences of a Nonagenarian.*

Ericson, Jack T., ed. *Folk Art in America: Painting and Sculpture* (Antiques Magazine Library). New York: Mayflower Books, 1979.

Evans, Nancy Goyne. "Documented Fraktur in the Winterthur Collection Part I," The Magazine *Antiques*, Vol. 103, no. 2 (February 1973), pp. 307–318.

————. "Documented Fraktur in the Winterthur Collection Part II," The Magazine *Antiques*, Vol. 103, no. 3 (March 1973), pp. 539–549.

Fabian, Monroe. "Research on the Pennsylvania German Kist," *Der Reggebage, Quarterly of the Pennsylvania German Society*, Vol. 6, no. 4 (December 1972), pp. 3–6.

Fales, Dean A., Jr., and Robert Bishop. *American Painted Furniture 1660–1880.* New York: E. P. Dutton, 1979.

Forbes, Harriette Meirifield. *Gravestones of Early New England and the Men Who Made Them.* Princeton, N.J.: Pyne Press, 1927.

Forman, Benno M. "The Crown and York Chairs of Coastal Connecticut and the Work of the Durands of Milford," The Magazine *Antiques*, Vol. 105, no. 5 (May 1974), pp. 1147–1153.

Garvan, Beatrice B., and Charles F. Hummel. *The Pennsylvania Germans, A Celebration of Their Arts 1683–1850.* (Exhibition Catalogue). Philadelphia: Philadelphia Museum of Art, 1983.

Gehret, Ellen J. "O Noble Heart…An Examination of a Motif of Design from Pennsylvania German Embroidered Hand Towels." *Der Reggebage, Quarterly of the Pennsylvania German Society*, Vol. 14, no. 3 (July 1980), pp. 1–15.

Greer, Georgeanna H. *American Stonewares, The Art and Craft of Utilitarian Potters.* Exton, Pa.: Schiffer Publishing, 1981.

Guiland, Harold F. *Early American Folk Pottery.* Philadelphia: Chilton Book Company, 1971.

Halsey, Abigail Fithian. *In Old Southampton.* New York: Columbia University Press, 1940.

Hansen, H. J. *European Folk Art.* London: Thames and Hudson, 1967.

Holstein, Jonathan. *American Pieced Quilts.* New York: A Studio Book/Viking Press, 1972.

Hughes, Judith Coolidge. "Sailors' Valentines," The Magazine *Antiques*, Vol. 79, no. 2 (February 1961), pp. 187–189.

Katzenberg, Dena S. "Baltimore Album Quilts" (Exhibition Catalogue). Baltimore: The Baltimore Museum of Art, August, 1981.

Kauffman, Henry. *Pennsylvania Dutch American Folk Art.* New York: Plantin Press, 1946.

Kaye, Myrna. *Yankee Weathervanes.* New York: E. P. Dutton, 1975.

King René's Book of Love. (Le Cueur d'amour espris). New York: George Braziller, 1980.

Kline, Robert M., and Frederick S. Weiser. "A Fraktur-Fest." *Der Reggebage, Quarterly of the Pennsylvania German Society*, Vol. 4, no. 34 (September–December 1970), 2–12.

Krueger, Glee. *A Gallery of American Samplers: The Theodore H. Kapnek Collection.* New York: Dutton Paperbacks in association with the Museum of American Folk Art, 1978.

————, *New England Samplers to 1840.* Sturbridge, Mass.: Old Sturbridge Village, Inc., 1978.

Larcom, Lucy. *A New England Girlhood: Outlined from Memory.* Cambridge, Mass.: The Riverside Press, 1889.

————. *To Cut, Piece, and Solder.* Lewisburg, Pa.: The Oral Traditions Project of the Union County Historical Society, 1982.

Lasansky, Jeannette. "Unusual Pennsylvania Ironware," The Magazine *Antiques*, Vol. 119, no. 2 (February 1981), pp. 438–444.

Lawrence, Henry. *The Not-Quite Puritans.* Boston: Little, Brown, 1928.

Lee, Ruth Webb. *A History of Valentines.* New York: The Studio Publications, 1952.

Lichten, Frances. *Folk Art Motifs of Pennsylvania.* New York: Hastings House, 1954.

————. *Folk Art of Rural Pennsylvania.* New York: Charles Scribner's Sons, 1946.

Lipman, Jean, and Alice Winchester. *The Flowering of American Folk Art, 1776–1876* (Exhibition Catalogue). New York: The Viking Press in cooperation with the Whitney Museum of American Art, 1974.

Little, Nina Fletcher. *Country Arts in Early American Homes.* New York: E. P. Dutton, 1975.

_____. *Neat and Tidy: Boxes and Their Contents Used in Early American Households.* New York: E. P. Dutton, 1980.

Ludwig, Allan J. *Graven Images: New England Stonecarving and Its Symbols.* Middletown, Conn.: Wesleyan University Press, 1966.

Meadows, Cecil A. *Trade Signs and Their Origin.* London: Reading & Fakenham, 1957.

Morse, John D., ed. *Country Cabinetwork and Simple City Furniture.* Charlottesville, Va.: The University Press of Virginia, 1969.

Northend, Mary Harrod. *Memories of Old Salem: Drawn from the Letters of a Great-Grandmother.* New York: Moffat, Yard and Company, 1917.

Orlofsky, Patsy, and Myron Orlofsky. *Quilts in America.* New York: McGraw-Hill, 1974.

Peesch, Reinhard: *The Ornament in European Folk Art.* New York: Alpine Fine Arts Collection, Ltd., 1983.

Rawson, Marion Nicholl. *When Antiques Were Young.* New York: E. P. Dutton, 1931.

Robacker, Earl F., and Ada F. Robaker. "The Far from Lonely Heart," *Pennsylvania Folklife,* Vol. 17, no. 2 (Winter 1967).

Schiffer, Margaret B. *Historical Needlework of Pennsylvania.* New York: Charles Scribner's Sons, 1968.

Sebba, Anne. *Samplers: Five Centuries of a Gentle Craft.* London: Thames and Hudson, 1979.

Shaffer, Ellen. "Fraktur: The Colorful Art of the Pennsylvania Germans," The Magazine *Antiques,* Vol. 95, no. 4 (April 1969), pp. 550–555.

Shelley, Donald A. *The Fraktur-Writings on Illuminated Manuscripts of the Pennsylvania Germans.* Philadelphia: Pennsylvania German Society, 1961.

Smith, Richard Flanders. *Pennsylvania Butter Molds.* Ephrata, Pa.: Science Press, 1970.

Sprackling, Helen. *Customs on the Table Top.* Meriden, Conn.: The Meriden Gravure Company, 1958.

Staff, Frank. *The Valentine and Its Origin.* New York: Frederick A. Praeger, 1969.

Stoudt, John Joseph. *Pennsylvania Folk Art.* Allentown, Pa.: Schlechter's Press, 1948.

Swan, Susan Burrows. *American Needlework.* New York: A Winterthur Book/Crown, 1976.

_____. *Plain and Fancy.* New York: A Rutledge Book/Holt, Rinehart and Winston, 1977.

Swarzenski, Hanns. "Two Oliphants in the Museum," *Bulletin of the Museum of Fine Arts,* Vol. 60, no. 320, 1962.

Tashjian, Dickran, and Ann Tashjian. *Memorials for Children of Chance.* Middletown, Conn.: Wesleyan University Press, 1974.

Teleki, Gloria Roth. *The Baskets of Rural America.* New York: E. P. Dutton, 1975.

The Book of the Dead, Facsimile of the "Papyrus" of Ani in the British Museum. London: Harris & Son, 1890.

The Gift of Inspiration: Shaker and American Folk Art. (Exhibition Catalogue). Hirschl & Adler Galleries, Inc., New York City, May 3–May 25, 1979.

The Secular Spirit: Life and Art at the End of the Middle Ages (Exhibition Catalogue). New York: E. P. Dutton in association with The Metropolitan Museum of Art, 1975.

Thiselton-Dyer, T. F. *Folklore of Women.* Williamstown, Mass.: Corner House Publishers, 1975.

Trent, Robert F. *Hearts and Crowns.* New Haven, Conn.: New Haven Colony Historical Society, 1977.

Watkins, Lura Woodside. *Early New England Potters and Their Wares.* Boston: Harvard University Press, 1968.

Webster, Donald Blake. *Decorated Stoneware Pottery of North America.* Rutland, Vt.: Charles E. Tuttle, 1971.

Weiser, Frederick S. *Fraktur...Pennsylvania German Folk Art.* Ephrata, Pa.: Science Press, 1973.

_____. "From the Cradle to the Grave: Something about Pennsylvania German Personal Documents and Folk Art," *Pfalzer-Palatines.* Kaiserslautern, Germany: Heimatstalle Pfalz, 1981, pp. 375–389.

_____. "Piety and Protocol in Folk Art. Pennsylvania German Fraktur Birth and Baptismal Certificates." *Winterthur Portfolio,* Vol. 8, Charlottesville, Va.: University Press of Virginia, 1973, pp. 19–44.

_____, and Howell J. Hearney, comps. *The Pennsylvania German Fraktur of the Free Library of Philadelphia,* 2 vols., Breinigsville, Pa.: The Free Library of Philadelphia, 1976.

_____, and Mary Hammond Sullivan. "Decorated Furniture of the Mahantango Valley," The Magazine *Antiques,* Vol. 103, no. 5 (May 1973), pp. 932–939.

_____. "Decorated Furniture of the Schwaben Creek Valley," in Albert F. Buffington, *et al, Ebbes fer Alle-Ebber—Ebbes fer Dich: Something for Everyone—Something for You. Essays in Memoriam—Albert Franklin Buffington.* The Pennsylvania German Society, Breinigsville, Pennsylvania, 1980. Vol. 14, pp. 333–394.

Woodard, Thos. K., and Blanche Greenstein. *Crib Quilts and Other Small Wonders.* New York: E. P. Dutton, 1981.

A NOTE ABOUT THE AUTHORS

CYNTHIA V. A. SCHAFFNER and SUSAN KLEIN have for many years been
associated with the Museum of American Folk Art in New York City.
From 1971–78, Cynthia V. A. Schaffner worked as an editor at
Mademoiselle. Since then, her articles on American folk art and antiques
have appeared in *House & Garden, House Beautiful, Country Living,* and
The Magazine *Antiques,* and she has lectured on folk art at the
Cooper-Hewitt Museum. She lives in New York with her husband, Robert,
and their daughter, Hilary.
Susan Klein's articles on American folk art and antiques have appeared
in *Country Living* and The Magazine *Antiques,* and she has lectured on
folk art at the Metropolitan Museum of Art and the Cooper-Hewitt
Museum. She lives in New York with her husband, Robert, and
their sons, Andy and Jeffrey.

A NOTE ON THE TYPE

This book was filmset in Fairfield, a type face designed by the distinguished
American artist and engraver Rudolph Ruzicka (1883–1978). This type
displays the sober and sane qualities of a master craftsman whose talent has
long been dedicated to clarity. Rudolph Ruzicka was born in Bohemia, and
came to America in 1894. He designed and illustrated many books and was
the creator of a considerable list of individual prints
in a variety of techniques.

Composition by Haber Typographers Inc.,
New York, New York
Separations, printing, and binding by Dai Nippon
Printing Co. Ltd., Tokyo, Japan

Designed by Margaret McCutchson Wagner